DIVORCE: THINK FINANCIALLY, NOT EMOTIONALLY®

Divorce: Think Financially, Not Emotionally® is a wonderful guide for women seeking to secure their financial future. The book spans socioeconomic groups and delivers a message which is helpful to anyone making important life decisions in a rational and intelligent manner.

—*Laura A. Wasser, Divorce Attorney to the Stars, including Maria Shriver, Heidi Klum, Angelina Jolie, Christina Aguilera, Mariah Carey, Britney Spears, and many others.*

I wish I had this book when I was going through my divorce. It would have made the learning curve much less steep! Knowing Jeffrey's expertise, any woman, whether going through a divorce or not, can benefit from this book!

—*Sonja Morgan, star of* Real Housewives of New York

Over the years, I have helped New York City's Mayor Mike Bloomberg build several shelters for battered and abused women and their children, so I've seen firsthand the challenges these women face. This book is packed with practical advice for any woman who wants to better protect her assets during divorce, but it may be particularly valuable for women in abusive relationships, who typically find it more difficult to escape their situations and secure a sound financial future. What's more, Jeff Landers is donating a portion of the profits from this book to organizations helping women in abusive situations. I wholeheartedly applaud his efforts.

—*Liz Smith, Syndicated Columnist*

DIVORCE

THINK FINANCIALLY, NOT EMOTIONALLY®

What women need to know about securing their financial future before, during, and after divorce

Jeffrey A. Landers, CDFA™

Sourced Media Books, LLC

ISBN 978-1-937458-49-2
LCCN 2012947648

Visit www.sourcedmediabooks.com

DEDICATION

This book is dedicated to all the women I have known who have struggled to break free from difficult and often abusive marriages. Your courage and determination have inspired me not only to complete this endeavor, but also to establish my 501(c)(3) nonprofit charity, the Bedrock Divorce Fund For Abused Women, Inc.

SUPPORT ABUSED WOMEN

A portion of all profits from the sale of each book will be donated to the Bedrock Divorce Fund for Abused Women, Inc., a 501(c)(3) nonprofit charity whose mission is to help female victims of domestic abuse and the organizations that support them.

CONTENTS

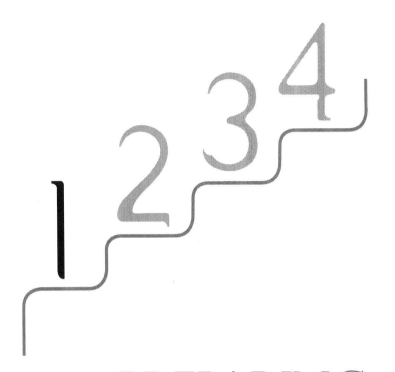

PREPARING
FOR DIVORCE

CHAPTER 1

INTRODUCTION

Divorce is an emotional rollercoaster. And if you're a woman who's going through or about to go through a divorce, you need to be keenly aware of this: People tend to make absolutely terrible financial decisions when they're on that rollercoaster, feeling "up" one minute and then "down" the next.

Of course, under the circumstances, a measure of indecision and confusion is completely understandable. If you're in the early stages of divorce, you're probably experiencing anger, betrayal, loss, shock, numbness, confusion, panic— or a combination of them all. It's no real surprise that you may not be able to think clearly about financial matters, such as how your assets might get divided, tax liabilities, and what your living expenses might be ten years from now.

But, here's the problem: When you're divorcing, you simply cannot risk being uninformed, indecisive, or bewildered about your finances. After all, the decisions you make both before and during your divorce will directly impact the rest of your life, for better or for worse.

If you proceed with your divorce carelessly and/or impulsively—allowing misinformation, rage, revenge, bitterness, depression, a lack of knowledge, or a sense of futility guide your decisions—the outcome can, and probably will, be financially disastrous. On the other hand, if you proceed thoughtfully and with a strategic plan, you may find your divorce offers you the opportunity to lock in a secure financial future.

The choice is yours, and the difference lies in how you handle the process and whether or not you can Think Financially, Not Emotionally®.

Someone once said that marriage is all about love, and divorce is all about money. She was right. And when you're going through divorce, you must keep your emotions in check, so you can negotiate a divorce settlement that financially protects you and your children both now and far into the future.

Unfortunately, thinking financially is not always easy, and this is true no matter how astute you are under "normal" circumstances. Many of our clients at Bedrock Divorce Advisors are accountants, lawyers, Wall Street executives, and business owners, some with Ivy League MBAs. These women know how to crunch numbers—but during the trauma of divorce, they just aren't able to focus and deal with financial matters.

No, thinking financially is not always easy. But, it *is* possible, especially if you have some help. Anyone, no matter how savvy, can benefit from expert advice when she is crossing through treacherous and unfamiliar territory. This book is a guidebook to help you navigate that difficult terrain.

Throughout the following chapters, I've compiled important information to help you better understand how to . . .

- ⇥ Shore up your financial position so you enter the divorce process prepared;
- ⇥ Gather your important financial documents and records;
- ⇥ Build a top-notch divorce team;
- ⇥ Determine the value of a small business or professional practice;
- ⇥ Decide between regular alimony and an up-front, lump-sum alimony payment;
- ⇥ Keep your marital house (if it makes financial sense to do so);
- ⇥ Get the child support you're owed;
- ⇥ Avoid the top mistakes divorcing women make;
- ⇥ Understand the difference between marital and separate property;
- ⇥ Protect any alimony and/or child support payments with life insurance;
- ⇥ Protect your business, intellectual property, and personal assets;

- ⇥ Divide your assets in a way most favorable to you from a tax and financial point of view;
- ⇥ Deal with pensions plans, 401(k)s, and other retirement accounts;
- ⇥ Decide whether to legally separate or divorce;
- ⇥ Disinherit your husband;
- ⇥ Determine if your husband is hiding assets;
- ⇥ and much more.

Ultimately, your goal should be to emerge from your divorce in the best financial shape possible. You're going to get off that emotional rollercoaster eventually. And when you do, you'll want to begin your single life knowing that you have made the thoughtful decisions required to help establish your long-term financial security.

Start today. Let me help you Think Financially, Not Emotionally® as you look ahead to a bright future for yourself and your children.

Note: This book is for informational purposes only and does not constitute legal advice. If you require legal advice, retain a lawyer licensed in your jurisdiction. The opinions expressed are solely those of the author, who is not an attorney.

A portion of the net proceeds from the sale of each book will be donated to the Bedrock Divorce Fund for Abused Women, Inc., a 501(c)(3) nonprofit charity whose mission is to help female victims of domestic violence and those organizations that support them.

CHAPTER 2

THREE REASONS YOU SHOULDN'T LISTEN TO DIVORCE ADVICE FROM FRIENDS AND FAMILY

Your friends and family care about you, and it's only natural for them to offer you support during your divorce. Sometimes, though, even the most well-intentioned advice from friends and family can cause confusion and unnecessary stress.

My clients at Bedrock Divorce Advisors tell me they hear it all. There's the best friend whose friend has yet another friend who knows a really good lawyer. There's the sister-in-law who knows "exactly" what you're going through—even though she has never been divorced. And don't forget the investment-savvy uncle who wants to fill you in on a little-known tip about how to handle your stock options; it worked for him, back in 1958.

How should you handle these situations? Should you act on the sincerely delivered advice of well-meaning friends, family, and/or non-divorce professionals? The answer is simple: No. Here's why:

1. **Every woman's divorce situation is unique.** Sure, it feels good to have those you care about rally around you. But given the complexities of today's divorce, tax, and finance laws, your break-up requires much more than an assortment of free tips and casual recommendations from friends and family, no matter how well-intentioned. And remember: Legal matters aren't the only complicated elements of divorce. Most couples' financial portfolios are incredibly complex, as well. Each divorce needs individualized, professional attention; and now, more than ever before, women need trained, experienced guidance to help ensure that they emerge from divorce with a comprehensive plan for a secure financial future.

2. **A little knowledge can be a very dangerous thing.** Many women who are going through divorce find themselves in particularly sticky situations because they have friends and relatives who work in legal or financial fields unrelated to divorce. Even though these friends and relatives may be highly intelligent, successful, well-meaning, and persuasive, listening to their advice about divorce will probably not help you. In fact, listening could hurt you.

   Let me give you an example. A family friend who specializes in business finance may be a genius in handling IPOs, corporate taxes, or mergers and acquisitions. But, it's unlikely that he has expertise regarding QDROs, the division of pensions, how to make long-term personal financial projections, and whether or not it's in your best interest to keep your marital residence. Likewise, a relative who's a CPA or an accountant may be very good at filing your taxes and giving you a snapshot of your present and past finances (balance sheet, profit and loss statements), but he or she may not be trained to calculate and project what your future financial positions will look like.

By the same token, financial advisors and stockbrokers shine at making investment recommendations but know absolutely nothing about the financial and tax implications of divorce. In fact, most financial advisory firms (Merrill Lynch, Morgan Stanley, Wells Fargo, etc.) prohibit their financial advisors/brokers from giving any advice on residential or commercial real estate and/or private businesses. They know they are not qualified to do so. In the end, other professionals have little or no idea what they are talking about, or what the law says, when it comes to the specific nuances that define a divorce.

3. **You can find the professional help you need.** There are about 3,500 Divorce Financial Advisors with the Certified Divorce Financial Analysts™ (CDFA) designation in the U.S. who are specifically trained in the financial aspects of divorce. What's more, many CDFAs have

completed additional education and training. For example, in addition to being a CDFA, I attended law school and completed dozens of advanced training courses in finance and divorce, including many of the same continuing education courses that are required for divorce and other attorneys (trust and estate, asset protection, etc.).

So, let those friends and relatives support you emotionally. Let them help you with your day-to-day concerns. But the next time they come forward to offer financial advice about your divorce, politely say, "No, thank you." Your future financial well-being is just too important to leave in the hands of Uncle Harry—even if he did hit it big on a stock market trade back in 1958.

Reminder: Because of their specialized training and experience, Divorce Financial Advisors are the most qualified and knowledgeable choice to help you work through the pros and cons of different divorce settlement proposals. By projecting the future financial and tax implications of each settlement option, CDFAs are the ones who can best show you whether your future is likely to be financially secure or not and thereby help you avoid the common, but often devastating, financial mistakes made in a divorce.

Hot Tip: Be judicious when discussing your divorce with family and friends. Keep in mind that every type of electronic communication has the potential to leave a digital trail—and that means your Facebook updates, your Tweets, your emails, your text messages, your blogs, and all your friends' and family's posts about you (including "incriminating" photos where you happen to be tagged) can and will be used against you. After all, your husband's divorce team wants to portray you in the worst possible way in hopes of bolstering his case. For example, if there's a photo online of you with a beer in each hand, it won't matter that one was for you and the other was for your friend. They'll try to convince the judge that you are an alcoholic and are therefore an unfit mother!

Legal Matters: A resounding 92 percent of the nation's top divorce attorneys say they have seen an increase in the number of cases using evidence taken from iPhones, Droids, and other smart phones during the past three years, according to a recent survey of the American Academy of Matrimonial Lawyers (AAML). In addition, nearly all (94 percent) of the respondents cited an overall rise in the use of text messages as evidence during the same time period. In other research, the AAML also found that social media sites now play a prominent role in many divorce cases. Overall, 81 percent of AAML members cited an increase in the use of evidence from social networking websites during the past five years. Nearly two-thirds (66 percent) of the AAML respondents reported Facebook as the primary source of this type of evidence. MySpace followed with 15 percent, Twitter with 5 percent, and other choices with the remaining 14 percent.[1]

---

1 AAML (2012). Facebook is primary source for compromising information. Press release, *PR Newswire*. Available at http://www.prnewswire.com/news-releases/big-surge-in-social-networking-evidence-says-survey-of-nations-top-divorce-lawyers-84025732.html?utm_expid=43414375-18.

CHAPTER 3

SIX FINANCIAL STEPS WOMEN MUST TAKE TO PREPARE FOR DIVORCE

The early stages of divorce are typically characterized by strong emotions such as betrayal, anger, shock, numbness, panic, and confusion. Regardless of who initiated the split or how long trouble was brewing in the marriage, the decision to proceed with divorce can still rock you to your core; and if you're like most women, you're now struggling with the nagging question, "What should I be doing to ensure the best possible outcome for me (and my children)?"

As a Divorce Financial Strategist™ who exclusively works with divorcing women across the country, my advice is to start organizing your personal finances right away. By taking a few relatively simple steps now, you'll undoubtedly save yourself many serious headaches later. Here's my short list of the six key financial steps you need to take as soon as you possibly can:

Collect Financial Documents

As I outline in this Divorce Financial Checklist, preparing for divorce requires gathering all the relevant documents related to your bank and brokerage accounts, credit cards, mortgages, tax returns, etc. Make copies of the year-end statements from these accounts so you can start tracking expenses, and then take all of these documents to a trusted friend/family member, or store them in a safe deposit box that your husband can't access.

Check Your Credit Report

Be sure to keep a watchful eye on your credit card statements, and if you haven't already done so, request a copy of your credit report. Once you have the report, monitor your score carefully so you'll be the first to know of any unusual activity. (Is your husband using your joint credit cards to take his girlfriend on a getaway vacation? Can you detect any other ways your husband is dissipating marital assets?) See my post, How To Protect Your Credit Score During Your Divorce, for more tips at www.bedrockdivorce.com/blog/?p=85.

Research Divorce Professionals

Don't attempt to tackle divorce on your own. Instead, take the time to build a qualified divorce team. I recommend you start with these three players: a matrimonial/family law attorney, a divorce financial planner, and a therapist/counselor.

Research the divorce professionals and create a short list of candidates for each position. Schedule interviews with each top contender to make sure you are comfortable with both their qualifications and their "bedside manner." By their nature, divorce proceedings are extremely intimate, and it's essential that you feel personally at ease with every member of your team.

Open New Accounts in Your Name

As a single woman, you'll need your own bank accounts and credit cards in your name—but opening these accounts is best accomplished while you are still married. Go to a bank where you don't have joint accounts with your husband, and open both a savings and a checking account. You'll need your own credit cards, as well, and starting that process now while you are still married is extremely important. New federal regulations are making it more difficult than ever for women with little or no income to establish credit on their own. So prepare yourself for the possibility that securing credit could be somewhat time-consuming and is likely to require more than simply filling out an application or making a single phone call.

Establish Private Communication

From the onset of your divorce proceedings, you'll need to correspond regularly with financial institutions, divorce professionals, and others—and you'll want that communication to be private. Many women find it beneficial to secure their own post office box for mail. (Just make sure you and perhaps a trusted friend or relative are the only one(s) with a key.) It's likely you'll also want a new, private email account and perhaps a new mobile phone, as well. (Please remember to reset the PINs/passwords on any of your old digital devices and accounts.)

Remain Vigilant

Is your husband explaining away mysterious purchases or time away from home—and dissipating family assets in the process? Is he dissipating assets through his business or professional practice? Be attentive; and if you are concerned at all about financial shenanigans by your husband, you may want to think twice about filing joint tax returns with him.

Reminder: Divorce is a journey. I know the idea of getting your personal finances in order can seem like a daunting task at first. But, as you work your way through this list, you'll realize that with each step taken, you'll be closer to having a stable and secure financial future as an independent woman.

Hot Tip: For many women, a comprehensive Lifestyle Analysis is an essential first step to assuming control of their personal finances. Prepared by a divorce financial advisor, a Lifestyle Analysis establishes what your standard of living was during the marriage. It reconstructs: 1) the day-to-day living expenses incurred during your marriage and 2) the spending habits of both you and your husband. The analysis will help determine how much you and your husband spent on an average basis month-to-month and year-to-year, and you can use these calculations as a guide to help you develop a budget for yourself as a single woman/mother.

Legal Matters: A Lifestyle Analysis serves as verification of net worth and the income and expense statements submitted by both spouses, and it can help a judge determine the amount of your divorce financial judgment, including the amount and duration of alimony. In many divorces, a Lifestyle Analysis is required by the court.

CHAPTER 4

GETTING ORGANIZED

For most women, going through divorce is like riding an emotional rollercoaster. Unfortunately, there are big downsides to experiencing so many ups and downs. It can be draining on you both physically and emotionally—and it can cloud your judgment, especially with regard to your personal finances.

Is there anything you can do to get off the rollercoaster? What steps can you take to regain a measure of control so you can Think Financially, Not Emotionally®?

Women ask me those two questions all the time, and I always give the same fundamental advice. The most basic step you can take towards getting the divorce settlement you deserve is to *get organized*. If you're organized, you'll have many of the facts, figures, and documents ready to hand over to your divorce team on day one. That means your divorce financial advisor can quickly, efficiently, and cost-effectively prepare a Lifestyle Analysis, a Financial Affidavit, and other needed analyses and projections. Then, based on these documents, your divorce attorney can get to work maximizing the amount of your temporary alimony and child support, and he/she can easily assess what additional information is needed during the discovery process.

There's no doubt about it: Being as prepared and organized as possible from the get-go often results in a less costly and overall better outcome. Plus, when you're intimately familiar with all the details in your case, you're more likely to give a better and more credible testimony should your divorce end up in court.

Here are a few simple steps you can take to become more strategic in your approach:

Collect Financial Documents

Gather all the relevant documents related to your bank and brokerage accounts, credit cards, mortgages, tax returns, etc. Year-end statements are particularly important. Make copies and take the copies to a trusted friend/family member, or store them in a safe deposit box that your husband can't access. For more details, see the Divorce Financial Checklist in appendix A of this book.

Have a Lifestyle Analysis Prepared

For many women, a comprehensive Lifestyle Analysis is the key to assuming control of their personal finances. Essentially, a Lifestyle Analysis establishes what your standard of living was during the marriage. It reconstructs: 1) the day-to-day living expenses incurred during your marriage and 2) the spending habits of both you and your husband.

The analysis will help determine how much you and your husband spent on an average basis month-to-month and year-to-year, and you can use these calculations as a guide to help you develop an accurate picture of what funds are required to maintain your standard of living. Of course, maintaining two households is more expensive than maintaining one, so it may not be possible to completely maintain your marital standard of living—but you'd like to get as close to it as possible.

Monitor Spending

Your Lifestyle Analysis will show you what funds came into the marriage (income) and what funds went out (expenses). Use this information to better plan your spending and to catch any red flags that may appear. Remember: Husbands hide assets (or, at least, try to hide assets) more frequently than most wives expect.

Secure Funds for Professional Fees

If your husband controls all access to the family funds, he can make it difficult (if not impossible) for you to have the resources necessary to hire the divorce team you need. Unfortunately, choking off the money supply is a common tactic, one that often forces a woman to sign a divorce settlement agreement that is totally lopsided in her husband's favor. Avoid this kind of financial squeeze. Be proactive. Make sure you have funds that are secure and available only to you.

Get Copies of Your Credit Report

By keeping an eye on your credit report, you'll know if your husband is charging gifts for his girlfriend on your joint credit cards, or if he's dissipating marital assets in some other way. Plus, you'll also be able to keep tabs on your all-important credit score.

Reminder: Everyone on your divorce team recognizes that this is a tremendously difficult time for you, and it's no surprise to anyone that you may not be able to think clearly about matters like the division of your assets and their tax implications or what your living expenses might be ten or twenty years from now. But *if you're well organized*, all the members of your team will be able to do their jobs faster, better, and more cost-effectively.

Hot Tip: Once you have hired a divorce team, opened new accounts in your name, etc., you'll be receiving mail that you will want to keep confidential. Before you do anything else, open a post office box and give yourself peace of mind knowing that your mail is being delivered to a secure, locked box that only you can access.

Legal Matters: A Lifestyle Analysis serves as verification of net worth and income and expense statements submitted by both spouses, and it can help a judge determine the amount of your divorce financial judgment, including the amount and duration of alimony. The court requires a Lifestyle Analysis in many divorces. Most states won't allow you to completely disinherit your husband until after the divorce is final. However, if you make changes to your will, medical directives/ living will, etc. now, you can prevent him from making medical decisions on your behalf or inheriting *all* of your assets should you die before the divorce agreement is signed. Eventually, you'll also want to change beneficiaries on life insurance policies, IRAs, etc.

CHAPTER 5

FOUR DIVORCE ALTERNATIVES

No two marriages are the same, so it follows that no two divorces are the same either. In fact, couples now have several options when it comes to choosing *how* they want to get divorced. In general terms, there are four broad categories of divorce alternatives: Do-it-yourself (DIY) divorce, mediation, collaborative divorce, and litigation.

Do-It-Yourself Divorce

The best advice I can give you about a do-it-yourself divorce is this: **DON'T** do it yourself!

Divorce is very complicated, both legally and financially. You can easily make mistakes, and often those mistakes are irreversible. The only scenario in which I could envision a do-it-yourself divorce possibly making sense would be in a case where the marriage lasted only two or three years, there were no children, there were few assets/debts to be divided, both parties had comparable incomes, and there would be no alimony. In a case like that, a do-it-yourself divorce could be accomplished quite quickly and inexpensively. Nevertheless, I would still highly recommend that each party have his or her own separate attorney review the final documents.

Mediation

In divorce mediation, a divorcing couple works with a neutral mediator who helps both parties come to an agreement on all aspects of divorce. The mediator may or may not be a lawyer, but he or she must be extremely well-versed in divorce and family law. In addition, it is critical for the mediator to be neutral and not advocate for either party. Both parties still need to consult with their own, individual attorneys during the mediation and prior to signing the final divorce settlement agreement.

Here are a few pros and cons to consider before deciding if mediation will work for you. On the "pro" side, divorce mediation may:

- Result in a better long-term relationship with your ex-husband, since you will not "fight" in court.
- Be easier on children, if the divorce proceedings are more peaceful.
- Expedite an agreement.
- Reduce expenses.

- Help you stay in control of your divorce because you are making the decisions (and the court isn't).
- Allow for more discretion. Mediation is private; litigated divorce is public.

On the "con" side, divorce mediation may also have the following consequences:

- Waste time and money. If negotiations fail, you'll need to start all over.
- Be incomplete or unduly favorable to one spouse. If the mediator is inexperienced or biased towards your husband, the outcome could be unfavorable for you.
- Result in an unenforceable agreement. A mediation agreement that's lopsided or poorly drafted can be challenged.
- Lead to legal complications. Any issue of law will still need to be ruled upon by the court.
- Fail to uncover certain assets. Since all financial information is voluntarily disclosed and there is no subpoena of records, your husband could potentially hide assets/income.
- Reinforce unhealthy behavior patterns. If one spouse is dominating and the other is submissive, the final settlement may not be fair.
- Fuel emotions. Mediation could increase negative behavior of a spouse with a propensity for physical/mental or drugs/alcohol abuse.

Couples often hear about the wonders of mediation and how it is reportedly a less contentious, less expensive, and more "dignified" way to get a divorce. However, my biggest problem with mediation is that the sole role and goal of the mediator is to get the parties to come to an agreement—*any* agreement! Remember, the mediator cannot give any advice. All he/she can do is try to get you to agree. Unfortunately, not all agreements are good agreements; in fact, in many cases, no agreement is better than a bad agreement. So unless both parties can be fairly reasonable and amicable (and if they can be, why are they getting divorced?), I believe that mediation is usually not a viable option for most women.

Collaborative Divorce

Simply put, collaborative divorce occurs when a couple agrees to work out a divorce settlement without going to court.

During a collaborative divorce, both you and your husband will each hire an attorney who has been trained in the collaborative divorce process. The role of the attorneys in a collaborative divorce is quite different than in a traditional divorce. Each attorney advises and assists his or her client in negotiating a settlement agreement. You will meet with your attorney separately, and you and your attorney will also meet with your husband and his attorney. The collaborative process may also involve other neutral professionals, such as a divorce financial planner who will help both of you work through your financial issues and a coach or therapist who can help guide both of you through child custody and other emotionally charged issues.

In the collaborative process, you, your husband, and your respective attorneys must sign an agreement that requires that both attorneys withdraw from the case if a settlement is not reached and/or if litigation is threatened. If this happens, both you and your husband must start over again and find new attorneys. Neither party can use the same attorney again!

Even if the collaborative process is successful, you will usually have to appear in family court so a judge can sign the agreement. But the legal process can be much quicker and less expensive than traditional litigation if the collaborative process works.

Unfortunately, I have found that the collaborative method often doesn't work well to settle divorces involving complicated financial situations or when there are significant assets. In collaborative divorce, just as in mediation, income, assets, and liabilities are disclosed voluntarily. Often, the husband controls the "purse strings," and the wife is generally unaware of the details of their financial situation. When this kind of inequality exists, the door is often wide open for the husband to hide assets. What's more, many high net worth divorces involve businesses and professional practices where it is relatively easy to hide assets and income. Additionally, the issue of valuation can be quite contentious.

Litigated Divorce

Most divorcing couples today choose the "traditional" model—litigated divorce.

"Litigated" does not mean the divorce ends up in court. In fact, the vast majority of all divorce cases (more than 95 percent) reach an out-of-court settlement agreement. *"Litigation"* is a legal term meaning "carrying out a lawsuit."

Why are lawsuits a part of divorce? Because contrary to popular belief, divorce usually does not involve two people mutually agreeing to end their marriage. In 80 percent of cases, the decision to divorce is unilateral—one party wants the divorce and the other does not. That, by its very nature, creates an adversarial situation right from the start and often disqualifies mediation and collaborative divorce, since both methods rely on the full cooperation of both parties and the voluntary disclosure of all financial information.

Clearly, if you are starting out in an adversarial and emotionally charged situation, the chances are very high that collaboration or mediation will fail. Why take the risk of going those routes when odds are they will waste your time and money?

The most important and most difficult part of any divorce is coming to an agreement on child custody, division of assets and liabilities, and alimony payments (how much and for how long). Although you want your attorney to be a highly skilled negotiator, you don't want someone who is overly combative, ready to fight over anything and everything. An overly contentious approach will not only prolong the pain and substantially increase your legal fees, it will also be emotionally detrimental to everyone involved, especially the children. Most divorce attorneys, at least those whom I would recommend, strive to come to a reasonable settlement with the other party. But if they can't come to a reasonable settlement, or if the other party is completely unreasonable, then going to court may be the only way to resolve these issues.

If you have tried everything else and you do end up in court, things can get really nasty and hostile. Once in court, the role of an attorney changes from "negotiator" to "litigator." Negotiations and compromise move to the back burner. Your attorney's job is now to "win" and get the best possible outcome for you.

At the end of the day, it's a judge who knows very little about you and your family that will make the final decisions about your children, your property, your money, and how you live your life. That's a very big risk for both parties to take—and that's also why the threat of going to court is usually such a good deterrent. Even so, litigation tends to yield the best possible outcome for most women going through divorce. When it comes to deciding whether to do it yourself, use mediation, participate in a collaborative divorce, or litigate, make sure that you weigh the pros and cons carefully with your divorce team.

Reminder: Weigh divorce options carefully. The bottom line is that every family, and thus every divorce, is different. Obviously, if you are able to work with your husband to make decisions and both of you are honest and reasonable, then mediation or the collaborative method may be best. But, if you have doubts, a litigated divorce will most likely serve you best.

Hot Tip: As a general rule, do NOT use do-it-yourself, mediation, or collaborative divorce methods if a) you suspect your husband is hiding assets/income; b) your husband is domineering and you are afraid to speak up; c) there is a history or threat of domestic violence (physical and/or mental) towards you and/or your children; and d) there is a history of drug/alcohol addiction.

Legal Matters: Most divorce attorneys, at least those whom I would recommend, strive to come to a reasonable settlement with the other party. But if they are unable to achieve this, going to court might be the only way to resolve these issues.

CHAPTER 6

FOUR KEY PLAYERS EVERY WOMAN NEEDS ON HER DIVORCE TEAM

Proceeding ahead with a divorce isn't easy. At times, it can seem like a potential pitfall is lurking around every corner. But, there is one thing you can do to substantially increase your odds for a successful outcome: *Build a winning divorce team.*

Do you really need a "team" approach? Yes, absolutely. Years ago, divorce was a relatively routine transaction involving only the divorcing couple and their lawyers. But now, the process is much more complicated. These days, you need the support of other professionals, particularly those who can help secure your financial interests both in the short- and long-term. To protect your financial stability and personal well-being, build a solid divorce team that includes four essential players: a family law attorney, a divorce financial planner, a therapist/counselor, and—the most important team member—you!

Matrimonial/Family Law Attorney

Choose an attorney who exclusively handles divorce cases or devotes at least 75 percent of his or her practice to divorce. Ideally, your lawyer will be a Fellow of the American Academy of Matrimonial Lawyers, an organization requiring the fulfillment of several stringent professional conditions.

When interviewing potential candidates for this position, make sure you take the time you need to thoroughly research their different practices. Certainly, you'll want to discuss the individual complexities of your case, but be sure to explore each lawyer's own qualifications and fees, as well. Honesty and openness are the best strategies here because there's no need for any "surprises" once you've started working together. Find out answers to questions like these:

- How many cases has he or she recently handled? How many have been settled, and how many have gone to trial? What were the outcomes of these cases?
- Does he or she typically represent the husband or wife? What percentage of each?
- Will he or she personally handle all aspects of your case, or will your case be passed to a more junior attorney and/or paralegal (and at whose rate will you be charged)?

In addition, be certain you feel personally at ease with whomever you choose. By its very nature, divorce is an intimate and emotional experience, and you need your attorney to be a trusted, supportive, and forward-thinking resource throughout the entire process.

Divorce Financial Planner

You're probably familiar with financial advisors, financial planners, CPAs, and accountants. But a divorce financial planner is something different—and even among divorce financial planners, you'll find different levels of training and expertise.

At a minimum, your divorce financial planner should have the Certified Divorce Financial Analyst™ (CDFA) designation, which shows that he or she has a more complete understanding of (and specialized training in) divorce. In addition, the ideal divorce financial planner will also have advanced training in divorce financial planning strategies and asset protection. My company's CDFAs with advanced training are called Divorce Financial Strategists™.

Think of a Divorce Financial Strategist™ as the financial expert on your team. He or she works hand in hand with your attorney to take care of the critical financial tasks beyond the capability of the divorce attorney's expertise. These tasks can range from preparing financial affidavits to creating the comprehensive financial analyses and projections that you and your divorce attorney will need to fully understand the short- and long-term financial and tax implications of each proposed divorce settlement offer. Your attorney will then use those conclusions to substantiate and justify his or her positions when negotiating with your husband's attorney or, if necessary, in court.

In certain circumstances, your divorce financial planner may also need to call in additional specialists, such as the following:

A forensic accountant can help explore concerns about hidden income/assets/liabilities and/or the possible dissipation of marital assets. He or she may also be very useful when one or both spouses own a business or professional practice, where it is rather easy to hide income/assets and/or delay revenues and increase expenses.

A valuation expert can determine the worth of a business or professional practice by using the "real" numbers as determined by a forensic accountant. A valuation expert can also establish the value of an advanced degree or training, stock options, and/or restricted stock.

A real estate appraiser can calculate the value of the marital home and other real estate, including vacation homes, commercial real estate, and land.

Therapist or Counselor

Many people describe divorce as an emotional rollercoaster, and at times, it can be difficult to navigate the ups and downs of the process. Because of this, your team should also include a qualified therapist who can help you cope as the divorce process unfolds.

You

Naturally, you are the most essential component of your divorce team—and even though this is an incredibly stressful time for you, you'll need to bring your "A" game. It's imperative for you to maintain your focus and Think Financially, Not Emotionally®. Treating the divorce as a business negotiation—which, in all honesty, is exactly what it is—will help you reach a divorce settlement agreement that financially protects you now and well into the future. In other words, you'll need to keep your cool under pressure. You'll need to learn how to delegate responsibilities to other members of your team so you can direct your time and your energy towards taking care of yourself and your family. And, you'll need to keep your sights set firmly on the future.

Reminder: You may be going through a very rough patch now, but ultimately, you and your children will be okay. There *is* life after divorce, and a strong divorce team will help you make that transition successfully. With the proper planning and support, your single life will be not only productive and fulfilling, but financially secure and stable, as well.

Hot Tip: Although you cannot deduct the cost of your divorce attorney and other expenses directly related to your divorce, you *may* be able to deduct certain fees and expenses for professionals who help you prepare your taxes. Also, keep in mind that professional advice may be able to save you thousands of dollars in the taxes you owe.

Legal Matters: Even meeting with an attorney for just a single initial consultation establishes an attorney-client relationship that cannot be breached. So, once you give an attorney details about your divorce, that particular attorney cannot be hired to represent your husband. This is called "conflicting out an attorney" and is a tactic often used by husbands to prevent their wives from hiring the best attorneys in town.

CHAPTER 7

PROTECTING
YOUR CREDIT

Your financial future as a single woman depends on a good credit rating, so it's critical that you take steps now to protect your credit score. Here are some tips for effectively handling joint credit cards and other debts so that your credit score is protected.

Get a Copy of Your Credit Report

You need your credit report for two main reasons: to find out your credit score and to check the report for inaccuracies.

The most commonly used credit score is FICO. To start the process, go to MyFico.com and request a copy of your credit information. Through MyFico.com, you can get reports from two of the three major credit-reporting agencies, Equifax and TransUnion. MyFico.com no longer provides credit reports from the third major credit-reporting agency, Experian, so you'll need to contact the company directly at Experian.com. There are many companies that offer credit reports, and some will provide them for free, but only MyFico.com will give you the all-important FICO score.

In addition to your credit score, your credit report will show you all the debts belonging to you and all those that you have jointly with your husband. You need to start closely monitoring accounts your husband has access to (credit cards, bank loans, mortgages, home equity lines of credit, etc.), so you'll know if there's unusual activity that may indicate he's dissipating or hiding assets, taking out loans, and/or obtaining credit. If you are concerned that your husband might try to borrow money in your name, you can sign up for a credit monitoring service. This service will notify you anytime there is a change to your credit history.

Close Joint Accounts with Creditors

Most likely, you will only be able to close accounts that have a zero balance. Nonetheless, you should call all credit card companies, banks, or other creditors to request that the account be closed—and make it clear that you will not be responsible for any charges. Follow up the phone call with a letter stating that you want the account closed. Keep a copy of the letter, as well as detailed notes of your phone conversation.

In both the phone conversation and the letter, ask that the lender report to the credit bureaus that the account was closed at your request.

Freeze Accounts That Can't Be Closed

If you aren't able to close an account due to an outstanding balance, request that a freeze be placed on the account. A freeze will prevent any further charges. You will still be jointly responsible for the balance, but no further debt can be added to the account. Remember to document all details related to this call and write and mail a letter.

Stay Current on Joint Accounts

Even though you are going through a divorce, it is very important to make payments to all joint accounts on time. Not making payments or paying late will hurt your credit score. Your credit rating will go down if a payment is missed or late—even if your spouse is assuming the debt.

Close Joint Bank Accounts

Most couples have joint checking and savings accounts. You need to close these as soon as possible, but talk to your lawyer before you do. Each state has its own specific laws governing how funds can be withdrawn from joint accounts when couples divorce.

Open New Accounts in Your Name

As a single woman, you'll need your own bank accounts and credit cards in your name—but opening these accounts is best accomplished while you are still married. Go to a bank where you don't have joint accounts with your husband, and open both a savings and a checking account. You'll need your own credit cards, as well, and starting that process now while you are still married is extremely important. New federal regulations are making it more difficult than ever for women with little or no income to establish credit on their own, so prepare yourself for the possibility that securing credit could be somewhat time-consuming and is likely to require more than simply filling out an application or making a single phone call.

Reminder: Your credit score is a number that is used to determine whether you are eligible for things such as a credit card, a loan to buy a car, a mortgage, etc. And, if you do qualify for a loan, your credit score can help determine what your interest rate will be.

Hot Tip: FICO credit scores in the U.S. typically range from 300 to 900, with the median at about 720. A score of 720 and above = excellent credit; 660 to 719 = good; 620 to 659 = fair; and 619 and below = poor. See www.creditcardforum.com/blog/

what-is-the-average-credit-score for more information.

Legal Matters: Even if your divorce settlement stipulates that your ex-husband is responsible for payment of certain debts you both entered into, if he does not pay them or declares bankruptcy, the creditors will come after you for payment! In other words, the creditors don't know and don't care what your divorce settlement says. If there is debt that you both entered into, you'll need to pay it if he can't or won't. You may want to include remedies in your divorce settlement to cover situations like this. For instance, you could make sure that joint assets are used to pay off all joint debt or have the property that is going to your ex-husband be placed in escrow until all debts are paid.

Legal Matters: Talk to your divorce attorney if you suspect your husband is using joint credit cards or other marital assets to travel with and/or buy gifts for a girlfriend. If your husband is dissipating marital assets, your divorce attorney will need to make that part of any discussion/negotiation.

DIVIDING ASSETS AND DEBTS: KEY CONCEPTS

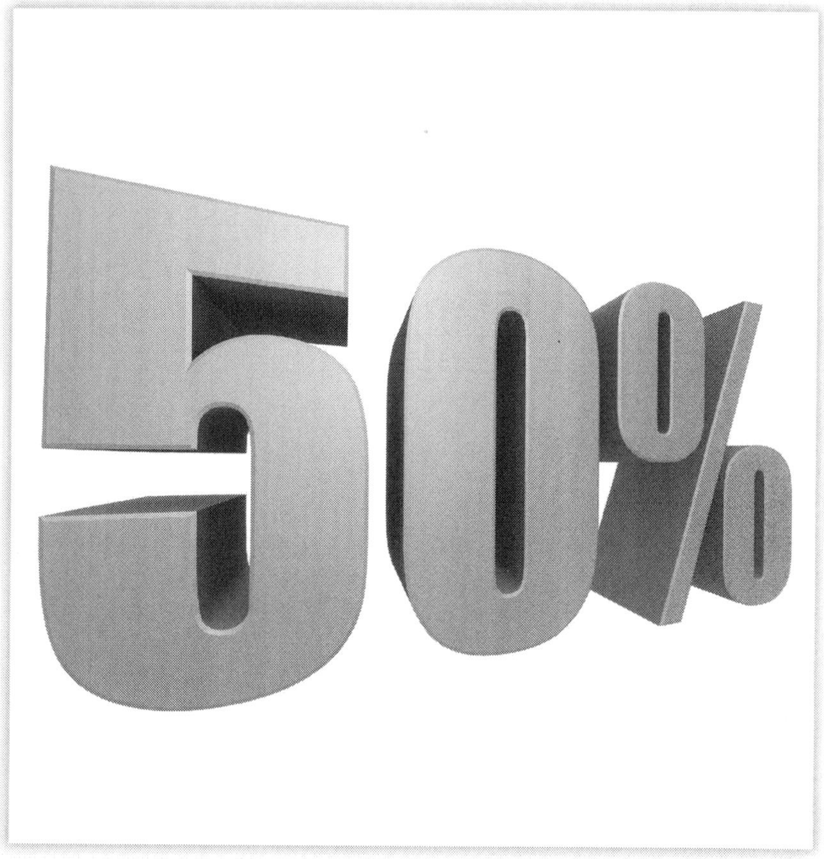
50%

CHAPTER 8

EQUITABLE DISTRIBUTION OR COMMUNITY PROPERTY?

Divorce laws differ from state to state, so *where* you live will impact *how* your assets and debts are divided in your divorce case.

First things first: You need to know whether you live in a community property state or an equitable distribution state.

There are nine **community property states**: Arizona, California, Idaho, Louisiana, Nevada, New Mexico, Texas, Washington, and Wisconsin.

The remaining 41 states are known as **equitable distribution states** (or common law states).

How do the asset distribution laws differ between a community property state and an equitable distribution state?

In a community property state, both spouses are typically considered equal owners of all marital property. In other words, if you live in a community property state, whatever you earn or acquire during the marriage is co-owned by both parties, regardless of who earned it or whose name is on the title. That means whatever you earn or acquire during the marriage is split 50-50 during a divorce.

If you live in an equitable distribution state, the law "sees" assets somewhat differently. In an equitable distribution state, if your name appears on an asset (e.g., the deed to a house or the title to a car), you are considered the owner. However, in an equitable distribution state, your spouse has the legal right to claim a fair and equitable portion of those assets in a divorce.

The equitable distribution of assets may result in a 50-50 split of marital property, or it may not. The goal in an equitable distribution state is not a 50-50 split. The goal is a fair (equitable) division of marital property.

A variety of different factors are considered when dividing marital property in an equitable distribution state. For example, equitable distribution may be based on:

- The length of the marriage.
- The age and health of the parties.
- The income and future earning capacity of the parties.
- The standard of living established during the marriage.
- The value of homemaking and childcare provided during the marriage.

- The value of the investment one party made to help with the education or training of the other party.
- Other factors.

Please keep in mind that the entire discussion above involves **marital property**. Separate property is a different matter (see chapter 9).

Whether you live in a community property state or an equitable distribution state, assets that you bring into the marriage or receive individually (e.g., an inheritance or your grandmother's diamond ring) remain yours. This separate property is exactly that—*separate*—unless you co-mingle it with marital property. For instance, if you deposited the inheritance from your parents into a joint bank account, it's likely that those funds would no longer be considered separate property. Once co-mingled, these funds could be considered marital property and subject to division as required by your state's laws.

In a nutshell, here's the difference between a community property state and an equitable distribution state:

- In a community property state, marital property is divided 50-50.
- In an equitable distribution state, marital property is divided equitably, based on a variety of factors.

Reminder: Assets aren't necessarily the only things acquired during marriage. Debt is often acquired, too. And just as assets are divided in divorce, debt is divided, as well. Generally speaking, the division of debt follows the same principles as the division of assets. For example, in most community property states, both spouses are equally responsible for the repayment of debt acquired during the marriage, even if only one spouse enjoyed the benefit. Also, debt often "travels" with the asset, so whoever gets the car also gets the car loan (and the same applies to real estate).

Hot Tip: Couples living in Alaska can "opt in" for community property, and Puerto Rico is a community property jurisdiction.

Legal Matters: A few states have laws with *both* community property and equitable distribution characteristics. Consult with your divorce attorney to learn which laws are specific to your state.

Legal Matters: You may be interested to know that the community property system is derived from Spanish law, and that's why it's found predominantly in the southwestern states.

CHAPTER 9

SEPARATE VS. MARITAL PROPERTY

In 2011, Arnold Schwarzenegger and Maria Shriver separated amidst a well-publicized scandal. The Governator then issued a statement that he was placing movie projects on hold to focus on personal matters. However, much more was at stake than his personal well-being. Under California law, all assets and income (including movie contracts) acquired after the date of separation are considered separate property that may not have to be divided. Did Schwarzenegger take time off for personal reasons? Perhaps. Did he delay signing contracts until they could no longer be considered marital assets? More likely.

Divorce involves dividing the family's property, and the process of deciding who gets what can be extremely complicated and contentious. The division of significant assets, such as houses, rental property, retirement/pension plans, stock options, closely-held businesses, professional practices, and licenses, is complex and often emotional, so you'll need to enter these negotiations prepared.

Let's start with the basics. One of the key factors divorcing women need to understand is *the difference between separate and marital property.* States differ in some of the details, but typically, **separate property** is rather limited in scope. Generally speaking, separate property only includes the following:

- Property owned by either spouse prior to the marriage.
- Property designated as separate property in a prenuptial or postnuptial agreement.
- An inheritance received by the husband or wife (either before or after the marriage).
- A gift received by the husband or wife from a third party (e.g., a diamond ring your mother gave you after you married).
- Payment received for the pain and suffering portion in a personal injury judgment.

All other property that is acquired during the marriage is usually considered marital property, regardless of which spouse owns the property or how the property is titled.

As you can see, compared to separate property, **marital property** is a very broad category.[2] Typically, all property that is acquired during the marriage is considered marital property, even if your spouse "owns" the property or it is titled in his name. So, don't think you're not entitled to a specific asset (such as a 401(k), stock options, etc.) simply because it is titled only in your husband's name—or because he tells you that the asset is related to his job and has nothing to do with you.

In fact, even separate property can lose its separate property status if it is co-mingled with marital property. For instance, if you re-titled the condo you bought when you were single and added your husband as a co-owner, that property would most likely be considered marital property. Likewise, if you deposited the inheritance from your parents into a joint bank account, it's likely that those funds would now be considered marital property.

Clearly, the division of assets can get quite complicated. But, don't feel overwhelmed. Take it step by step. Understanding the fundamentals of how assets are divided will help you feel more in control and start you on your way to a successful settlement.

---

2 Go to www.forbes.com/sites/jefflanders/2011/04/12/understanding-how-assets-get-divided-in-divorce/ to view an interactive chart outlining different types of marital property.

Reminder: Understanding the difference between separate and marital property is only the first step in approaching the division of family property. You must also recognize that divorce laws differ greatly from state to state. You need to know if you live in a community property state or an equitable distribution state, because where you live impacts how your assets and debts will be divided during divorce.

Hot Tip: Debt also needs to be divided when you divorce. Like assets, debt is handled in accordance with state laws, and community property states and equitable distribution states deal with debt quite differently.

Legal Matters: In many states, if your separately owned property increases in value during the marriage, that increase in value may also be considered marital property. The division of this particular subset of marital property can be further complicated by the difference between active and passive appreciation of the assets (see chapter 12).

CHAPTER 10

DATE OF SEPARATION

Women who are going through divorce typically have to field lots of questions from well-meaning friends and family. They want to know what happened, when you realized the marriage was truly over, what you did once you realized you were headed for divorce . . . and much more.

Perhaps drawing the proverbial line in the sand helps people cope with the break-up. Conversations, events, even emotions can be duly partitioned. "This" happened before the separation. "That" happened after.

In many ways, the courts want to be able to do the same thing. But, they are not interested in establishing a timeline for social or emotional reasons. Instead, the courts need to establish a formal Date of Separation (DOS) in order to determine various property interests and to establish valuation dates for certain assets.

The DOS matters because it draws a very significant line of demarcation. In general, all assets and income acquired from the date of marriage to the date of separation are marital property; anything acquired after the date of separation is separate property.

The implications can be dramatic. For example, the Date of Separation can be a major issue if one spouse is awarded a big bonus, commission, or stock options just after (or before) he or she claims to have separated from the other spouse. Unfortunately, pinpointing the actual DOS can be tricky.

Different states determine the DOS in different ways. In some states, the DOS is the date you and/or your husband physically relocate from the marital place of residence. Or, it can also be the date you physically separate, even if it's in the same house. (Maybe you sleep in the bedroom, while he sleeps in the den.) In other states, the DOS is the date on which one spouse officially informs the other that he or she intends to file for divorce.

Still others define the DOS as the date when the legal separation agreement is signed or the actual divorce papers are filed in a court of law.

Adding to the confusion, even some of these guidelines can be interpreted in different ways. Your husband could say he didn't believe you were "serious" the first time you informed him that you were going to file for divorce. Or, he could argue that he physically relocated but didn't formally change his address (or that it was only a trial separation, and neither party had any intention of divorcing at that time).

Determining the DOS can be complicated. But, once the date is established, you can start planning a strategy for a successful settlement.

Reminder: It makes sense to be judicious about the determination of the DOS. Obviously, you'll want the date to be most advantageous to you, so it's essential that you assemble a qualified divorce team to help you sort through all the particulars of your case.

Hot Tip: The DOS affects the division of debt, as well. You don't want to be responsible for the thousands of dollars in bills your husband starts racking up with his new girlfriend. Let's hope he doesn't start charging those trips until *after* the DOS!

Legal Matters: In divorce, the point in time in which an asset is assigned a dollar value is called its *valuation date*. In addition to determining various property interests, the DOS can also establish valuation dates for certain marital property assets. For some assets, the DOS and valuation dates will be the same. For others, the valuation date may be the Date of Trial.

CHAPTER 11

VALUATION DATES

Divorce requires the division of all your marital assets. For instance, you may want to keep the house, while he may be more interested in keeping the business. You'll have to decide how to split the stock portfolio, retirement accounts, the vacant beachfront property, the art pieces you bought together . . . and more.

How are these decisions made? Is there any way to ensure the division of marital assets is equitable? The answers to questions like those are generally quite complex. But, the process always begins the same way. The first step in the proper partitioning of marital assets is to assign each one of those assets an accurate dollar value—and since the value of certain assets can fluctuate, assets have to be assigned a value on a certain date. In divorce, the point in time when that dollar value is assigned is called its *valuation date*.

At first, that may sound relatively straightforward. Since each asset needs a dollar value, all you have to do is simply pick a date and value each item as of that date, right? Well, unfortunately, like most other aspects of divorce, the determination of valuation dates isn't typically straightforward at all. In fact, the process can be quite complex. Why?

For starters, as I mentioned, the value of an asset can significantly vary, depending on the date that is chosen to be its valuation date. Plus, each state has its own specific regulations and guidelines. For example, in New York, the court must select a valuation date as soon as possible after the divorce action has commenced. Other states may use the trial date, the date of separation, the date the divorce complaint was filed, or another date as the valuation date.

Valuation Date vs. Date of Separation

In the preceding chapter, I discussed why divorcing women need to pay careful attention to the date of separation (DOS). The DOS is important because it draws a very significant line of demarcation. It is the line in the sand between when you were married (and functioning as a couple) and when you were separated (and no longer functioning as a couple). Since the DOS can help determine the division between marital and separate property, it sometimes can be used to establish a valuation date.

In other words, in some cases, the DOS itself is used as the valuation date. But, in other cases, it's not.

Date of Separation vs. Trial Date

Generally, active assets are valued as of the DOS, while passive assets are valued as of the trial date.

An **active asset** is any marital property that can change in value due to the actions of its owner. For instance, a business, a professional practice, and even the marital home can be considered active assets. As a result, it makes sense for an active asset to be valued as of the DOS; otherwise, the spouse who controls the asset might allow its value to diminish as the divorce proceedings unfold.

A **passive asset,** on the other hand, is any marital property that can change value because of forces beyond the direct control of its owner. For example, vacant land and stock portfolios may be considered passive assets because their value depends on market forces. In this case, it makes more sense to value the asset at the trial date.

Impact of Valuation Dates

Assigning a valuation date can have a significant impact on the value of a particular asset. The easiest way for me to explain this is by using examples.

In a New Jersey appeals case, the husband owned a seat on the New York Stock Exchange. The seat nearly doubled in value between the time of the filing of the divorce complaint and the time of the divorce trial. Which date should be used as the valuation date? The courts ruled that the date of the divorce trial should be used as the valuation date. In this case, the increase in value was viewed as entirely passive, since it was not based on the actions of either party.

In other cases, different rules apply. For instance, a business that is managed by only one spouse is usually considered an active asset and would typically be valued as of the DOS (or commencement of the divorce action in New York). This approach makes sense for two reasons:

1. It protects the spouse who controls and manages the business. Should the value of that business increase between the DOS and trial date due to the efforts of the managing spouse, then that spouse should be awarded the benefits of his or her labor.

2. It protects the nonmanaging spouse. Should the spouse who controls and manages the business decide to run the business into the ground, the nonmanaging spouse should not suffer any loss as a result of the managing spouse's actions.

While the complexities surrounding the concept of a valuation date can seem a bit confusing, there is no need to worry as long as you have a divorce team to help you work through the specifics of your case. With their help, you'll be able to manage your assets and develop a comprehensive plan for continued financial stability and security in the future.

Reminder: Since there is often a long delay between separation and divorce, you'll want to work closely with your divorce team to help you work through the nuances of DOS and valuation dates so that, to the extent possible, you can use a valuation date that is the most advantageous to you.[3]

Hot Tip: A volatile economic climate can make the determination of valuation dates even more complicated. For example, a judge may rule that any decrease in the value of a business was a result of the recession and had nothing to do with the actions of the managing spouse. In essence, the judge could deem a normally active asset (the business) to be a passive asset and therefore would use the trial date as the valuation date rather than the DOS (or commencement of the divorce action in New York).

Legal Matters: State laws vary greatly. Please consult with your divorce team to determine how DOS and valuation dates are determined in your state. (The complexity of assigning a valuation date is nicely illustrated in a list of each state's laws found at the following url: www.divorcesource.com/tables/valuationdate.shtml.)

---

3 Divorce Source (2012). Separation. Available at http://www.divorcedex.com/divorce/Separation-1111.shtml.

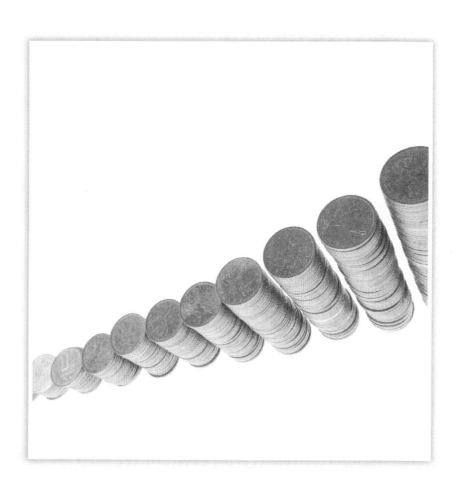

CHAPTER 12

ACTIVE VS. PASSIVE APPRECIATION

After reading about the difference between separate and marital property, you're probably starting to make mental lists. Maybe those lists are even titled: "Mine," "His," and "Ours."

While it makes perfect sense for women who are going through divorce to start thinking in those terms, you also have to remember this: The lines between the categories "Mine," "His," and "Ours" often get blurry; and odds are, you will encounter a few financial nuances as your divorce proceedings unfold.

For example, it's possible your case will involve separate property that has appreciated in value during the course of your marriage. But even though the asset may be separate property, should that appreciation be considered marital property or separate property? What's more, how is that appreciation defined? Is it active or passive appreciation?

So, what is the difference between active and passive assets? An asset can increase in value in one of two ways. An asset can either:

- ❧ **Actively appreciate**, as a result of actions by the owner of the asset, or

- ❧ **Passively appreciate**, as a result of changes in the market.

While there are many complex rules that govern division of property and asset appreciation, below are a few fundamentals, in very general terms:

In community property states, where both spouses are typically considered equal owners of all marital property, the division of appreciated assets is often computed based on a series of formulas. The calculations can prove enormously complex, but here's a short summary of the most salient points by David M. Wildstein, Esq. in his brief, *Allocating Active and Passive Appreciation of a Separate Business Asset for Equitable Distribution*:

> If the increase in a separate asset is passive, it is not a part of the community estate as long as no community resources were used for the asset. If the asset increases due to the effort of either party, it is part of the community. The time, toil and talent of each spouse is perceived to be a community asset. To reach a fair result, community property law created the doctrine of reimbursement: 'The fundamental purpose

of the doctrine is to bring back into the community estate value which was created by community contributions, but which took the form of appreciation in the value of a separate asset.'[4]

In equitable distribution states, it's not as clear-cut, because none of the equitable distribution states use a formulaic approach as described above for community property states. In equitable distribution states, passive appreciation on separate property remains separate property. But, active appreciation on separate property can be considered marital property.

What can qualify as active appreciation on separate property? That's a very good question, and courts often struggle to make this determination. Typically, the judge will use a three-pronged test to evaluate active appreciation in separate property. The judge must find that:

1. The separate property appreciated during the marriage.

2. The parties directly or indirectly contributed to the appreciation.

---

4 Wildstein, D. (2012). Allocating active and passive appreciation of a separate business asset for equitable distribution. Available at http://www.wilentz.com/Files/ArticlesandPublicationsFileFiles/42/ArticlePublicationFile/AllocatingActiveAndPassiveAppreciationOfASeparateBusinessAssetForEquitableDistribution.pdf

3. The appreciation was caused, at least in part, by the contributions.

As you can see, asset appreciation is a complicated topic that demands thorough and thoughtful consideration. It's essential that you seek guidance from a qualified divorce team concerning the particular circumstances of your individual case.

Reminder: There are nine community property states: Arizona, California, Idaho, Louisiana, Nevada, New Mexico, Texas, Washington, and Wisconsin. The remaining 41 states are known as equitable distribution states (or common law states).

Hot Tip: Typically, all property that is acquired during the marriage is considered marital property, even if your husband "owns" the property or it is titled in his name. So, don't think you're not entitled to a specific asset (such as a 401(k), stock options, etc.) simply because it is titled only in your husband's name, or because he tells you that the asset is related to his job and has nothing to do with you.

Legal Matters: The rules governing the determination of asset appreciation can vary from state to state. In some states, the burden of proof is on the spouse who claims the appreciation is passive. In other states, it's the reverse—the burden of proof rests on the spouse who claims the appreciation is active.

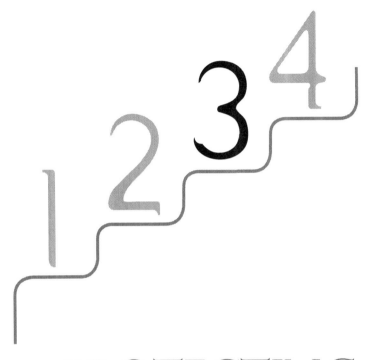

PROTECTING
YOUR ASSETS

CHAPTER 13

SHOULD YOU KEEP THE HOUSE?

My clients tend to fall into one of three categories when we start discussing whether or not they want to (or should) keep their marital residence.

- ↦ The first group sees the house as not just a piece of real estate, but as a *home* filled with family history and sentimental value.

- ↦ The second group feels quite differently. These women consider the house the center of painful memories and/or the root of financial trouble.

- ↦ The last group adopts a more matter-of-fact approach, seeing the marital residence as neither overwhelmingly positive nor negative. To them, the house is one of many assets to be negotiated in the divorce process.

Regardless of how *you* view it, your marital residence is likely to figure prominently in your divorce proceedings. Often, it's the biggest asset a couple owns together, and usually it comes fully furnished with all sorts of emotional trappings, as well.

Part of our job at Bedrock Divorce Advisors is to complete the financial analyses needed to help a woman understand if she can afford to own the house, and if so, for how long. One of the first steps in that process is determining the answers to a few fundamental questions. If you're divorcing and you think you would like to keep your marital residence, it's time for you to carefully consider the following questions:

Why are you interested in keeping the house? There are many practical and fair reasons to want to keep the house. Perhaps you're raising your children in this house, and it's near both school and work. Or, it could be a family home passed down from generation to generation. Just be sure that your list of reasons to keep the house isn't dominated by purely emotional ones. Remember: In order to reach a divorce settlement agreement that puts you on solid financial footing, you'll need to Think Financially, Not Emotionally®.

Can you afford to keep the house? Whatever your income level, this is a critically important question. House-related expenses can significantly impact your budget once you are single, so make sure you carefully consider all the costs associated with home ownership: mortgage payments, real estate taxes, utility bills, maintenance, repairs, landscaping and upkeep, etc.

Have you fully considered the true worth of the house vs. other assets? Not all assets that are valued the same are actually *worth* the same. Here's an example to illustrate my point:

Let's say you're trying to decide whether to keep a $600,000 bank account or a $600,000 house that's completely paid off. You really love the house, and you're leaning in that direction. Great idea? Maybe. But, you need to carefully assess how the house will impact your bottom line—both now and years down the road. Even mortgage-free home ownership involves expenses, such as real estate taxes that need to be paid every year, upkeep and maintenance, fuel costs, etc. In addition, when you eventually sell your home, you may be hit with a big capital gains tax bill. Let's assume you bought the home for $200,000, and it's now worth $600,000. Your capital gain is $400,000. Subtract your $250,000 capital gains exclusion as a single person, and you'll have to pay capital gains tax on $150,000. At the current capital gains tax rate of 15 percent, that amounts to a $22,500 tax bill! (And chances are pretty good that those tax rates will increase in the near future.)

Once you complete this type of analysis, the cash may look like a much better option than the house.

What other living options are available to you? It's only natural to feel a sentimental attachment to the place where you live. But don't become so entrenched that you fail to recognize viable alternatives. Perhaps it's a good idea to downsize. Or maybe, when it comes right down to it, you would actually prefer a different neighborhood? Could a new home give you that feeling of a clean slate? Odds are that even if you weren't divorcing, you would eventually move from your current residence. Though it may not seem like it at the time, there are many different places you could call "home."

Could the proceeds of selling your house create new opportunities and allowances? Selling or downsizing could open new doors for you and your family. These new proceeds could be turned into an investment, a retirement fund, reserves for your children's future education, or simply extra financial security to depend on if another curve ball comes your way. In the end, knowing that these new options are now true possibilities may be more valuable than the house, despite attached sentimental value.

Reminder: Maintaining emotional distance when it comes to negotiating your marital house won't necessarily be easy. But, if you can successfully do so, you'll put yourself in a better position to strategically manage your assets and develop a comprehensive plan for financial stability and security in the future.

Hot Tip: Even affluent women who own marital residences worth millions of dollars, mortgage-free, may have to sell their houses at some point. Why? Because, it's just not sensible to keep so much cash tied up in such a relatively illiquid investment (which, especially in this sluggish economy, may not increase in value for many years).

Legal Matters: When children are involved, the parent who is awarded custody often stands the best chance of being awarded the house, as well. Most courts want to minimize disruptions to children and family routines, if at all possible.

CHAPTER 14

RETIREMENT ACCOUNTS AND PENSION PLANS

Contrary to popular belief, young couples aren't the only ones who go through divorce. In fact, a recent study showed that between 1990 and 2009, the divorce rate among older adults actually doubled. In 2009, about one in every four divorces occurred among people over the age of 50.[5]

When you're a woman who's 50+ and divorcing, there's no question that retirement accounts, pension plans, and Social Security will factor significantly into your divorce settlement agreement—but even if you're *not* nearing retirement age, the same is likely true. For many couples, retirement accounts and/or pension plans represent a considerable chunk of their

5 Brown, S. (2012). The gray divorce revolution: Rising divorce among middle aged and older adults, 1990-2009. Institute for Population Research. Retrieved August 23, 2012 from http://ipr.osu.edu/events/susan-brown-bgsu-gray-divorce-revolution-rising-divorce-among-middle-aged-and-older-adults-19.

net worth, and as such, they all must be addressed in divorce settlement agreements. Unfortunately, though, dividing retirement accounts and pension plans is very complicated, fraught with many tax implications, and often mishandled (since many lawyers don't have sufficient expertise in this area).

So, if you're divorcing, remember to Think Financially, Not Emotionally® and keep the following key elements top of mind regarding retirement accounts and pension plans.

1. Retirement funds added during the marriage are typically treated as marital property. While you are married, it's only natural for you and your husband to plan for retirement together. Contributions to 401(k)s are made via deductions from salary, and pension plan benefits are a function of years on the job and salary earned. It makes perfect sense that you start counting on that money for when you and your husband reach your Golden Years.

Obviously, divorce changes every one of those plans and requires the careful scrutiny of all retirement accounts.

For example, retirement funds added during your marriage are typically treated as marital property. However, if a spouse enters the marriage with money already in his/her 401(k), those funds are considered separate property and, as such, are not included in the division of assets. (However, in some states, any increase in value of separate property during the term of the marriage is considered marital property; see chapter 9.)

Any retirement assets that qualify as marital property can be divided, but the process by which these funds are divided depends upon a number of factors. For starters, the court must adhere to federal guidelines when dividing funds in 401(k), 403(b), and other similar types of plans, but state laws dictate how IRAs are divided. It's critical that your divorce settlement agreement clearly spells out how the assets are split and how those funds will be transferred. There are even more thorny issues to contend with when you need to divide a pension plan.

2. Division of a 401(k) plan and many pension plans require a Qualified Domestic Relations Order (QDRO). If your divorce settlement agreement states that you will divide a pension and/or 401(k) plan, a court must order a Qualified Domestic Relations Order, commonly abbreviated as QDRO (pronounced "Quad Row"). A QDRO will instruct the plan administrator on how to pay the non-employee spouse's share of the plan benefits. A QDRO allows the funds in a retirement account to be separated and withdrawn without penalty and deposited into the non-employee spouse's retirement account (typically an IRA).

Many women (and some attorneys, too!) often make the mistake of assuming that their divorce settlement agreement will fully protect their rights to their portion of a husband's retirement account. This is usually not the case, and that's why it's critically important to use a properly prepared QDRO.

The QDRO must be completed and presented to the pension plan well before your divorce is finalized. Waiting to complete the QDRO until after the divorce is finalized is recipe for disaster! Imagine a scenario in which the divorce has been finalized and the QDRO requires the pension plan to pay an immediate lump-sum amount to the non-employee spouse (typically the woman). Let's further imagine that the non-employee spouse was relying on that lump-sum payment to pay legal fees and other immediate expenses.

The reality is that many pension plans will not pay a lump-sum amount and will only pay the non-employee spouse on a monthly basis for life starting at around retirement age, which could be many years in the future. Under these circumstances, the QDRO requesting the immediate lump-sum payment would be rejected by the pension plan.

If that's the case, the spouse who was counting on receiving immediate cash to pay legal fees and other bills is in for a major disappointment. Since the divorce has already been finalized, the non-employee spouse cannot go back to the court and request some other property (cash, stocks, etc.) that would have an equivalent value to that anticipated lump-sum payment. The non-employee spouse is now out of luck and may have to wait decades to start collecting a share of the monthly pension payments.

On the other hand, if the QDRO had been completed and presented to the pension plan well before the divorce was finalized, the non-employee spouse could have negotiated a different settlement with more cash, for example, once he or she found out that an immediate lump-sum payment from the pension would not be possible.

Another disastrous scenario would be if the employee spouse died between the time the divorce was finalized and the approval of the QDRO by the pension plan. After the divorce, the employee-spouse would be considered single and his/her monthly pension payments would be calculated on a single life basis. Therefore upon the death of that employee spouse, any payment obligations of the pension fund would disappear. The non-employee spouse would not be entitled to anything. Once again, this problem could be avoided by making sure that the QDRO was completed and presented to the pension plan well before the divorce was finalized.

3. A QDRO specialist will help you avoid costly mistakes. At first, the topic of how retirement accounts and pension plans are divided in divorce may make your head swim. There are a tremendous number of factors and implications to consider—and essentially, you have only one chance to get it right.

Well, let me clarify. You have one chance to get it right per pension plan. A separate QDRO is required for each pension plan, 401(k), etc. So, for example, if you have a pension plan, a 401(k) from your current job, and a 401(k) from a previous job, three separate QDROs are required.

Because QDROs are so complicated to prepare, it's not surprising that most attorneys now outsource their preparation to a QDRO specialist. If you're divorcing, please make sure this important step does not fall through the cracks and that the QDRO is issued as close to the time of divorce as possible. Otherwise, you could jeopardize your standing and, under certain circumstances, lose all rights to certain retirement funds.

Reminder: When it comes to divorce, the best defense is a good offense. To help ensure you have a financially secure retirement, take protective measures while you're married. Even happily married women need to preserve a measure of financial independence, and it's essential that you keep a separate bank account, establish credit in your own name, maintain access to all marital money, divorce-proof your business, etc.

Hot Tip: If your ex-husband is at least 62 years old and is now receiving Social Security benefits, you are entitled to half of these benefits, provided that: 1) You were married to him for at least ten years. 2) You are now at least 62 years old. (If your ex is deceased, you can start collecting at age 60.) 3) Your Social Security benefits under your own work record are less than his. (You can only receive one Social Security benefit.) 4) You are not currently married. Your benefits do not reduce your ex-husband's benefits in any way. If you meet the requirements above, your ex will receive 100 percent of his benefits, and the government will pay you 50 percent of the amount he receives, as well.

Legal Matters: A Qualified Domestic Relations Order (QDRO) is required if your divorce settlement agreement states that you will divide a pension and/or 401(k) plan. However, a QDRO is not necessary to divide an IRA or a SEP. Military pensions and federal, state, county, and city retirement plans have their own rules regarding division during divorce.

CHAPTER 15

UNDERSTANDING ALIMONY

I'm an advocate for alimony. If a woman has been in a long-term marriage and has either been out of the work force for decades or has an income that is substantially less than her husband's, I firmly believe she needs—and deserves—alimony in order to maintain a post-divorce lifestyle that's at least somewhat comparable to the lifestyle she enjoyed while married.

Of course, I also believe the same applies for a man who is divorcing under similar circumstances. Any ex-husband who has stayed out of the work force, has less income, etc., needs—and deserves—alimony, as well. (In fact, alimony laws in most states are gender neutral and apply equally to husbands and wives.) However, in the vast majority of cases, it's typically ex-wives who receive alimony payments.

What's the purpose of alimony?

The purpose of alimony (also called "spousal support" or "maintenance") is to somewhat equalize the economic disparity between a husband and wife. I feel a woman deserves alimony if she has income that is substantially less than her husband's, and she:

➻ sacrificed her educational opportunities, potential career, and earning power so she could invest her time and labor for the betterment of her family.

➻ directly or indirectly aided her husband's career by taking care of the home front and enabling him to invest in his job opportunities and increase his earning power.

➻ helped her husband (financially or otherwise) complete law school, medical school, or other professional training.

Let's face it. In many instances, a marriage ends when the husband is at or near the peak of his earning power (thanks in part to his wife). And if the wife has sacrificed education and job opportunities to help him advance his career and/or raise children, her earning power has likely diminished, and she may be relatively unemployable.

Keep in mind that alimony payments are not assigned arbitrarily. They are almost always determined by both the payor's ability to pay and the payee's need; and beyond that, more and more state laws now specify that the term of alimony must be directly related to the length of the marriage.

Can't the division of assets make up the difference?

Even though a divorcing couple may divide assets 50-50, the husband, because of his earning power, will often replace some or all of those assets over time, while the wife, because of her lack of earning power, will often need to start liquidating assets from day one. Alimony helps to somewhat equalize this economic disparity.

Why doesn't a woman just go back to school and then find a job?

Even when the economy is healthy, it's not easy for older women who have been out of the workforce for decades to get "re-educated" and find a job. In a shaky economy, that task is even more difficult. In fact, research shows that unmarried women now experience high and extended unemployment, as well as underemployment. Older women face even more challenges.

Are there different types of alimony?

Yes, there are a variety of different alimony alternatives, and it's essential for you to find the one that best suits your needs. For the moment, let's focus on these two options:

➻ **Regular alimony (or periodic alimony)**
➻ **Up-front lump-sum payment**

Regular alimony is paid in established intervals (typically monthly) and usually continues per the divorce settlement agreement until: 1) the spouse who's receiving it remarries (or, in some cases, cohabitates); 2) either party dies; or 3) either party goes to court to seek a modification (either an increase or a decrease) based on a substantial change in financial circumstances.

Let me repeat item number three above: With regular alimony, either party can go to court to seek a modification (either up or down) based on a substantial change in financial circumstances.

Of course, any modifications to alimony, child support, and/or other divorce-related payments must be approved by the court. However, if the judge agrees that the ex-husband can no longer afford to pay the current amount of alimony, that judge can decide to reduce those required payments.

What can you do to protect yourself from this kind of economic uncertainty? For me, the answer to that question is straightforward. If you want to protect yourself from the economic uncertainties of regular alimony, you should pursue an up-front lump-sum payment in lieu of alimony.

An up-front lump-sum payment in lieu of alimony is a one-time payment of a fixed amount unaffected by any future changes in your ex-husband's financial status. In other words, any ex-wife who agrees to a lump-sum payment will not be particularly worried about the effects of economic uncertainty on her ex-husband's income. She will receive everything she is entitled to at once, and her ex-husband cannot come back to request any modifications.

I recommend an up-front lump-sum payment in lieu of alimony for most of my clients; but before I do, I must be certain that:

- There are sufficient assets available to make such a lump-sum payment.

- The recipient is not a spendthrift.

- The recipient has no lawsuits pending against her.

- The recipient has good continuing financial advice about asset protection and how to make the lump-sum payment, along with the rest of her settlement, last as long as possible.

At Bedrock Divorce Advisors, we've seen how devastating it can be for a woman to lose her alimony income, but an up-front lump-sum payment can prevent that kind of financial trauma from happening. Of course, because the entire alimony payment is made all at one time, an up-front lump-sum payment requires careful, deliberate financial management. As mentioned above, you will have to handle the one-time payment appropriately so that it sustains your lifestyle long-term.

Reminder: Child support payments or property settlements (i.e., payments that do not qualify as alimony) are always nondeductible to the payor and nontaxable to the recipient. However, alimony is different, and both the payor and the recipient need to abide by the tax regulations that govern all alimony payments. Keep the following in mind:

1. The federal tax treatment of alimony is governed by the Internal Revenue Code, *not* by divorce agreements or court orders. However, your divorce agreement should state whether or not the parties agree that alimony payments are tax-deductible to the payor and taxable income to the recipient. (Yes, you can agree that alimony payments will not be tax-deductible for your husband and taxable income to you!)

2. In general terms, alimony is typically taxable income for the recipient and a tax deduction for the payor.

Hot Tip: Even if you do choose to accept periodic alimony payments, there are ways to help protect yourself from economic uncertainties. For instance, any woman who plans to accept periodic alimony payments should establish a life insurance policy to secure alimony payments and enable her to receive a tax-free, lump-sum payment of what she would have received over time from her alimony, child support, and/or other divorce-related payments should her ex-husband die.

If you choose to take this route, it's best to establish this life insurance policy before the divorce has been finalized. After the divorce, your ex-husband may refuse to cooperate in getting the required medical exam, or you may discover during the process that he is uninsurable. Either way, you need to know this before the divorce is settled so that, if necessary, you can find alternate ways of securing your divorce settlement payments.

Legal Matters: Each alimony alternative has its own specific tax implications. For example, since an up-front lump-sum payment in lieu of alimony is usually structured as part of the division of assets, it is not taxable to the recipient or tax deductible to the payor. Because the payor will lose those tax deductions, he will rightfully want to discount the amount of the lump-sum payment to be made. (Count on your divorce financial expert to help you make those calculations.)

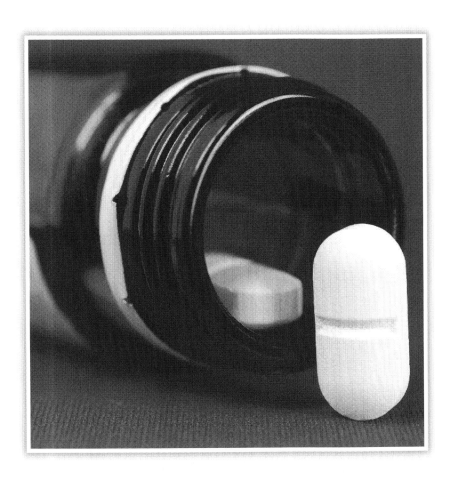

CHAPTER 16

HEALTH INSURANCE, LIFE INSURANCE, AND SOCIAL SECURITY

Most married couples don't spend much time thinking about their health insurance policies, life insurance policies, and Social Security accounts. Once established, these fundamental elements of a couple's financial portfolio typically run on auto-pilot, carrying on month after month and going largely unnoticed.

But, of course, all that changes when you decide to divorce. Once divorce proceedings commence, every marital asset must be analyzed, assessed, and divided; and if you're wondering how the division of marital assets will impact your health insurance policy, your life insurance beneficiaries, and your Social Security account after you divorce, let me offer some guidance.

While each divorce is unique and deserving of the attention of a qualified divorce team, here are some general answers to the three questions my clients ask most frequently about health insurance, life insurance, and Social Security.

Can I stay on my ex's health insurance plan after we divorce?

The laws regarding health insurance are straightforward, and the answer to this question can be summed up in a single word: No. Once divorced, you *cannot* stay on your ex's health insurance—but your children *can* and probably should (although who will pay the premiums for them could be a topic for discussion).

Once the divorce is finalized, you (the non-employee spouse) can qualify for COBRA coverage, but remember: COBRA is temporary and lasts only up to 36 months. In order to qualify for COBRA, you must notify your plan administrator within 60 days after divorce or legal separation, and then your plan administrator must give notice (generally within 14 days) to you about the right to elect COBRA continuation coverage. Keep in mind that the group health coverage under COBRA is likely to be more expensive than what you have been paying, since the employer typically pays part of the premium for active employees, while COBRA participants generally pay the entire premium themselves, plus an administrative charge of two percent.[6]

---

6 See the guide, *How to Calculate Your Monthly COBRA Insurance Cost*, for more details. Available at http://www.cobrainsurancebenefits.org/How-to-Calculate-Your-Monthly-COBRA-Insurance-Cost.php.

Maintaining health insurance coverage is a major concern for many divorcing couples; in fact, it's one of the main reasons that some couples now opt for a legal separation instead of divorce. But, if you do decide to legally separate rather than divorce, please tread carefully. Some health insurance companies view a legal separation as essentially the equivalent of divorce, so they will not continue coverage for a separated spouse.

Can my husband remove me as beneficiary of his life insurance policy?

There are two specific time frames when there is a simple one-word answer to this question. Yes, your husband certainly can remove you as beneficiary of his life insurance policy if:

- the divorce action has not yet commenced, or
- your divorce has been finalized.

However, if you are *in the process* of getting a divorce, the answer is not so straightforward. For example, many states impose an Automatic Temporary Restraining Order (ATRO; see chapter 21) on couples who are in the process of getting a divorce. This ATRO prohibits either party from changing beneficiaries, modifying accounts, selling or mortgaging property, etc., without the consent of the other party and/or the court.

Dig a little deeper, and you'll see that the issue of life insurance can become even more complex once the discussion broadens to include factors such as alimony and child support. Why? Because life insurance policies are often used to secure alimony and child support payments.

In other words, if your ex-husband is the one paying alimony and/or child support, the court may require him to maintain a life insurance policy as a way to guarantee he will uphold these mandated payments. The time frame for this type of obligatory life insurance will vary, depending on the duration of the alimony and child support agreements.

And that's not all. I also advise my clients to consider life insurance from yet another angle. Once again, if your ex-husband is the higher earner who is paying alimony and/or child support, I highly recommend that you purchase a life insurance policy on him in order to secure these important divorce settlement payments. This life insurance policy must be established *before* your divorce has been finalized, *and* you should be both the owner of the policy and the beneficiary—because that way you can be sure that the premiums will be paid on time and the beneficiary won't be changed without your knowledge and consent.

Why should I get life insurance?

Remember, most of your divorce settlement payments (alimony, child support, etc.) will end upon the death of your ex-husband. The proceeds from the life insurance policy can ensure you receive a tax free, lump-sum payment of what you would have received over time from your divorce settlement payments.

Why before the divorce is finalized?

If your husband refuses to cooperate in getting the required medical exam, or if he is uninsurable due to health or other reasons, you need to know this before the divorce is finalized so you can find an alternate way of securing your divorce settlement payments.

I can only scratch the surface here, but I hope I've made it clear that: 1) life insurance is a very complex topic, and 2) the laws and regulations differ from state to state. Beneficiaries cannot be re-designated after the insured's death, so please consult your divorce financial expert before proceeding, weigh your options carefully, and make sure all policies are kept current. If your ex "forgets" to pay his premiums, the entire policy could be at risk.

Am I eligible for a portion of my ex-husband's Social Security benefits?

If your ex-husband is at least 62 years old and is now receiving Social Security benefits, you are entitled to half of these benefits provided that:

➤ You were married to him for at least ten years.

➤ You are now at least 62 years old. (If your ex is deceased, you can start collecting at age 60.)

- Your Social Security benefits under your own work record are less than his. (You can only receive one Social Security benefit.)
- You are not currently married.

Your benefits do not reduce your ex-husband's benefits in any way. If you meet the requirements above, your ex will receive 100 percent of his benefits, and the government will pay you 50 percent of the amount he receives, as well. Note: If your ex-husband predeceases you, you are eligible to the entire benefit. And, if your ex-husband dies, any of his children under the age of 18 (or 19 if they are full-time students) are eligible for benefits, as well.

Reminder: If you're divorcing, it's only natural for your thoughts to be swirling with questions regarding important issues, such as health insurance, life insurance, and Social Security. Hopefully, the answers above will help you gain some needed perspective. After all, when you're divorcing, it's critical for you get the facts so you can Think Financially, Not Emotionally® and achieve the divorce settlement agreement you need for a solid, stable financial future.

Hot Tip: Even if life insurance policies are not being used to secure alimony and child support, many couples revise their policies so that their children are the beneficiaries. If your children are minors, you can appoint an adult custodian to receive and handle the benefits on their behalf or, better yet, put the life insurance in a special trust called an ILIT (Irrevocable Life Insurance Trust).

Legal Matters: Be certain to check with your health plan provider regarding the specific regulations and restrictions that apply to your policy. Health insurance companies have stringent requirements for when and how they must be notified of your divorce, and failure to do so could constitute insurance fraud. Your attorney can help you understand the laws as they apply to your specific case.

CHAPTER 17

PROTECTING YOUR BUSINESS

Whether you're a successful female business owner or a woman who's part of a successful family business team, you've undoubtedly sacrificed an enormous amount and spent untold hours to make the business thrive. Does the end of your marriage mean the business has to come to an end, as well?

No. Divorce does not have to mean the end of a family business. But, it can put your ownership stake in the business at risk—and that's true whether or not your husband was directly involved in the company and regardless of who initiated the divorce.

Take, for example, the case of Frank and Jamie McCourt. Together, they owned and operated the L.A. Dodgers. But when they divorced, a costly legal battle ensued, threatening the existence of the Dodgers itself. They eventually settled in what is known as the costliest divorce in California's history:

Jamie received $130 million, but Frank gained full control of the Dodgers.[7] So, what can you do to protect your business once you and your husband decide to split up? Keep these five recommendations in mind:

1. Determine whether the business is separate or marital property.

Details differ from state to state, but separate property typically includes the following:

- Property owned by either spouse prior to the marriage.
- Property designated as separate property in a prenuptial or postnuptial agreement.
- An inheritance received by you or your husband (either before or after the marriage).
- A gift received by either spouse from a third party (e.g., the diamond ring your mother gave you).
- Payment received for the pain and suffering portion in a personal injury judgment.

All other property that is acquired during the marriage is usually considered marital property, regardless of which spouse owns the property or how the property is titled.

---

7 Boeck, S. (2011). Dodgers' McCourts reach divorce settlement. *Arizona Business and Money*, October 17. Retrieved August 1, from http://www.azcentral.com/business/articles/2011/10/17/20111017D odgers-McCourts-reach-divorce-settlement.html#ixzz21ESWkpfy.

So, in very general terms, if your business was started before the marriage, the value of the business at the time of marriage will usually be considered separate property. In contrast, any increase in value between the date of marriage and the date of separation might be considered marital property, depending on whether that appreciation was active or passive. (Where you live will determine how any active or passive appreciation of separate property should be treated.)

If your business was started after you married, it would typically be considered marital property and be included as part of the marital assets that must be divided between you and your husband.

2. Pay attention to other states' laws.

Each state has its own set of laws governing the division of a family business in divorce. There are nine community property states—Arizona, California, Idaho, Louisiana, Nevada, New Mexico, Texas, Washington, and Wisconsin—and in these states, both spouses are usually considered equal owners of all marital property. (That means, in these states, a 50-50 split is the rule.)

The remaining 41 states are equitable distribution states, where several other factors, such as the length of marriage, age and health of the parties, income, and future earning capacity, are considered when determining a settlement. Settlements in equitable distribution states do not need to be equal, but they should be fair (equitable).

3. Establish the true value of the business.

As part of your divorce team, a valuation expert can determine the value of the business. This analysis can tell you the value of the business at different points in time (e.g., at the time of marriage, on the date of separation, etc.) and can be used to substantiate and justify your position when negotiating with your spouse's attorney. If the business is owned and/or operated by the husband, a forensic accountant is often brought in to determine the real income and expenses of the business prior to its valuation. In many cases, the forensic accountant and the valuation expert are the same person. This is especially important if there are any red flags that indicate there might have been some financial shenanigans on the part of the husband.

4. Carefully consider all your options.

In general terms, the options for dealing with a family-run business fall into five broad categories. You can:

- ↦ Continue with the status quo. Both you and your spouse maintain your current roles in the business.

- Transition to new roles. You may have to change individual responsibilities and/or hire new employees.

- Decide that only one spouse will keep the business. The other spouse is then compensated with an appropriate buy-out. (For example, you could pay off your husband with a Property Settlement Note, which allows for a long-term payout with interest of the amount you owe your ex-husband for the value of his share of the business.)

- Sell the business and divide the profits.

- Form an Alimony and Maintenance Trust (also known as a Section 682 Trust) or some other type of trust. An Alimony and Maintenance Trust can be funded by the business owner with equity in the family business (or other income-producing assets). As a result, the income generated by the equity interest can be used to pay the former spouse for his share of the family business. An Alimony and Maintenance Trust may be desirable when 1) a business owner does not want to (or can't) sell an interest in a business to make divorce settlement payments, 2) the business lacks the liquidity to redeem the stock of the former spouse, or 3) you need an alternative to a Property Settlement Note (as described above).

5. Divorce-proof your business while you're single or happily married.

Tips 1–4 are designed to help you better understand the circumstances surrounding the division of a family-run business during divorce. However, it's much, much easier to prepare for the possible division of a family-run business before your marriage hits the skids—or even better, before you're married.

There are several approaches you can take to protect your business—so female business owners, please take note. For instance, you can:

- Use a prenuptial or postnuptial agreement.
- Establish a Domestic or Foreign Asset Protection Trust (or another type of trust).
- Create a buy-sell or operating agreement (something that every business with more than one partner/owner should absolutely have).

Remember, though, in order for them to be legally effective, many of these protections must be in place years before the possibility of divorce is even on the horizon. Obviously, a prenuptial agreement needs to be signed before you are married, and something like a transfer to an irrevocable trust must be done *years* in advance. In some states, transactions can be voided up to seven years after the transfer.

Whether you are about to be married or are in the thick of divorce proceedings, there are steps you can take to preserve your business. Work with your divorce team to ensure that the option you choose is the right one for you and your circumstances.

Reminder: According to the Small Business Association, 90 percent of all U.S. businesses are family-run. If you're divorcing, make sure you protect your business interests and Think Financially, Not Emotionally®. With a qualified divorce financial planner on your team, you'll be able to carefully consider your options and plan for a stable and secure financial future.

Hot Tip: Many states still don't recognize postnuptial agreements. Even in the states that do, they are frequently challenged and often invalidated. Nonetheless, having a postnup in place is probably better than having nothing at all.

Legal Matters: The use of a Domestic or Foreign Asset Protection Trust does not preclude you from also having a prenup. However, in that case, the prenup might no longer need to address the issue of your separate property and its appreciation. Instead, it could purely focus on how marital property would be divided and who would receive alimony, in what amount, and for how long.

CHAPTER 18

INTELLECTUAL PROPERTY

Every few months, it seems there's a blaring new headline about a high-profile celebrity break-up that has become caustic and bitter. Some of these divorces are fought tooth and nail in the courts for months—or even years.

But, what exactly are these Hollywood couples fighting about? Are these contentious, protracted divorces really battles for who gets the bigger house, the more expensive car, or the most valuable artwork?

Well, yes, as with any divorce, the division of those kinds of assets certainly plays an important role. However, it may surprise you to learn that most celebrities aren't likely to spend months in court arguing about vacation homes and retirement accounts. Why not? Because celebrities realize they have something much more important to fight for. You see, the thing celebrities battle most about when they divorce is this: intellectual property rights.

Celebrity couples (and their attorneys) are well aware of the value of intellectual property rights. They know these rights can potentially be worth millions—and that's precisely why celebrity break-ups can be extremely combative.

For example, the divorce dispute between Michael Douglas and his first wife, Diandra, has been dragging on in the courts since 2000! In one of her more recent actions, Diandra filed suit in 2011 claiming that she is entitled to half of Michael's earnings from *Wall Street: Money Never Sleeps*, a film released in 2010. Why? Because in their initial divorce settlement, Michael agreed to pay Diandra half of the acting earnings he accrued while they were married, including any residuals, merchandising, and ancillary rights.

Reportedly, their agreement also contained language stating Diandra would be entitled to additional money from any future "spinoffs." According to her latest suit, Diandra contends the new film is a spinoff, since it involves a character Michael developed in the original *Wall Street* (which was filmed during their marriage). As a result, she claims she is entitled to half of his earnings from the new movie too. Michael's position is that the new movie is a sequel and *not* a spinoff, so Diandra isn't entitled to anything. As remarkable as it sounds, Diandra's entire case now revolves around this single, seemingly picayune point: Is the new movie a spinoff or a sequel? If it's a spinoff, she gets half. If it's a sequel, she gets nothing. Picayune or not, the resolution of this point could be worth millions . . . and once again, it all hinges on intellectual property rights.

Should you be fighting for your intellectual property rights too?

If you're considering divorce, there are a few essential points you need to know to better understand how the split could impact your intellectual property.

First, let's be clear about who may have intellectual property. If you're an author, songwriter, artist, poet, actor, designer (software, website, fashion, packaging, architectural, etc.); or, if you're an inventor, entrepreneur, or business owner; or, if you have a website, logo, tag line, articles, and/or white papers you've written, then you have intellectual property.

There are four main types of intellectual property:

1. Patents

2. Trademarks

3. Copyrights

4. Royalties and other contractual rights

Any of these types of intellectual property may be considered marital property, which means they may be divided during divorce.

Rules about how intellectual property can be divided vary from state to state, but the general rule of thumb is this: Value that's created during the marriage must be divided. And, by extension, any value that's created before or after the marriage is typically excluded from division.

In community property states, both spouses are usually considered equal owners of all marital property, so any value created from intellectual property would be split 50-50. If you live in an equitable distribution state, the division of marital property does not need to be equal (50-50), but it should be fair (equitable).

Regardless of what state you live in, what's referred to as "creative control" typically remains with the inventor or creator of the intellectual property. Think about it for a minute and you'll realize this is a reasonable approach—it usually maximizes future income potential, which obviously works in the best interests of both parties.

Reminder: Hollywood celebrities and high-profile executives aren't the only ones who own intellectual property. If you have been involved with nearly any kind of creative endeavor (you've written songs, started a business, designed a website, etc.), *you* may have intellectual property too. Make sure your intellectual property rights are protected during your divorce.

Hot Tip: If intellectual property is completed partially before the marriage and partially during the marriage, the rights will have both separate and marital components.

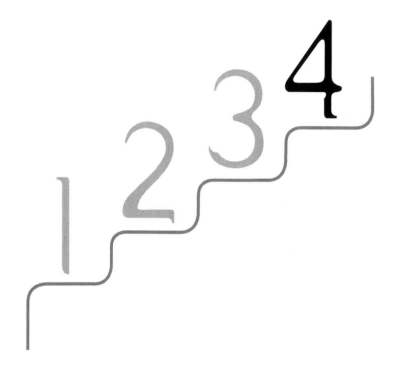

SPECIAL TOPICS

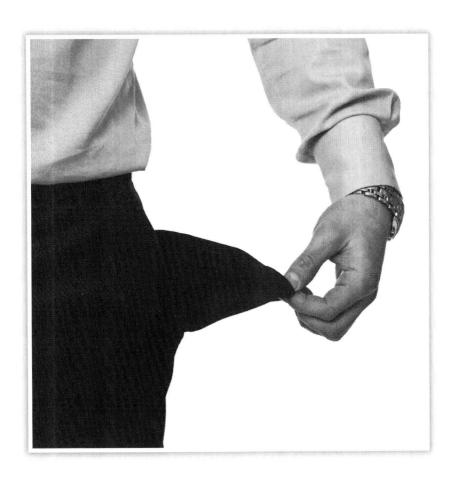

CHAPTER 19

EIGHT UNDERHANDED TACTICS HUSBANDS USE DURING DIVORCE

No woman likes to think her husband has dirty tricks up his sleeve. But pretending husbands never lie or cheat during divorce doesn't do anyone any good, either.

Divorcing women need to understand the full range of tactics some husbands use, and they need to be proactive, not reactive, as they work to secure the best possible divorce settlement.

Don't get me wrong. Not all divorces are bitter battles. Some are relatively amicable, and most of them are settled outside the courts. However, at Bedrock Divorce Advisors, we've seen quite a few underhanded financial and legal tactics employed by husbands or their divorce teams. Here are the top eight:

1. **"Conflict out" all the top divorce lawyers.** By "conflicting out" certain attorneys, your husband can make it difficult for you to hire the lawyer

that's best for you. Here's how this tactic works: Your husband makes appointments with all the top lawyers in your area. Then, he meets with each one—but only for a short time. All he needs to do during those meetings is share enough information to create an attorney-client relationship. Once he does, that particular attorney will be prohibited from representing you.

Of course, your husband doesn't actually have to hire any of these attorneys. The entire goal with this tactic is to "conflict out" attorneys so they cannot be hired by you.

The lesson here is simple. *Don't procrastinate when hiring a divorce attorney.* If you do, you could miss out on the opportunity to retain a great lawyer.

2. Stall and delay. By repeatedly rescheduling court hearings and/or filing excessive motions and requests for evidence, your husband can drive up your legal costs and stretch out the time during which you must cover living expenses. In these cases, he's hoping you'll run out of money and be forced to agree to his settlement offer, which is often extremely unfavorable to you.

3. Exert pressure to proceed too quickly. If your husband wants you to agree to a "quick" settlement, he may have something to hide. For instance, very early in the process, his attorney may send over a settlement proposal for you to review and counter. Usually, this means he just wants to get the divorce over and done with quickly, and he wants you to settle for what appears to be a reasonable offer. The problem is that in many cases, you will not receive all the discovery documents requested, so you won't have complete knowledge about key financial matters, such as marital assets, income sources, expenses, what you owe, and what is owed to you.

Rushing to get a settlement is especially sneaky if your husband has been busy hiding assets and/or income, and now he is trying to get you to agree to a 50-50 split of only a portion of your total assets!

4. Deny access to financial resources. Unfortunately, many married women do not take a hands-on approach to the family finances. During a divorce, your husband may use your lack of knowledge to his advantage. He can cut off your credit cards, move funds out of family accounts, ensure that only he can access family funds, etc. Actions like these can leave you without the money necessary to buy groceries, much less hire the right divorce team—while he hires an excellent team to represent him.

This is especially problematic for abused women who live in constant fear of harm to themselves and/or their children.

5. Hide assets. As I discuss extensively in the next chapter (see chapter 20), hiding assets during a divorce is sneaky, unethical, and illegal—but it happens much more frequently than most women realize.

6. Fail to pay court-ordered support or refuse to relinquish assets. If your husband doesn't follow court orders, he's breaking the law. But trying to extract the promised payments from him can come at considerable legal cost long after the divorce is over. In addition to the expense, all this financial and legal wrangling is terribly time-consuming. Some women have to take time off from work to deal with these issues, and that can put their jobs in jeopardy. Sadly, many family courts do a poor job enforcing such orders, even when a woman follows its requirements to the letter; additionally, deception on the part of an ex-husband can be difficult to decipher or prove, even for a well-meaning judge.

7. Falsely claim their wives are abusers. This ploy is just as ugly as it sounds. Some men are upending domestic violence laws so that their wives (who are the true victims) are arrested, prosecuted, and even sentenced as abusers. Unfortunately, these scams undermine sound public policy and create confusion that, paradoxically, ends up protecting abusers.

8. Use fraud or coercion to obtain credit using their wives' names. The abuser in a violent relationship may secretly open credit card accounts in the victim's name, trick the victim into relinquishing her rights to certain marital assets, coerce the victim into signing financial documents, and/or use any one of a number of other despicable tricks. As a result, the victims of coerced debt often are left with the devastating consequences of negative credit. They have difficulty opening credit card accounts, obtaining loans, renting, even finding a job—not to mention the time and expense required for credit repair.

Reminder: Keep your eyes open, and try to remain proactive, not reactive. During the divorce, you'll need to Think Financially, Not Emotionally® so you can keep your finances intact while planning for a secure financial future.

Hot Tip: Because there are so many different dirty tricks, I recommend that women maintain an emergency fund in a separate bank account, even if divorce has never entered their minds. If you are contemplating divorce, make sure you start organizing your personal finances and important documents under the guidance of a qualified divorce financial planner.

Legal Matters: Let me reiterate: *Don't procrastinate when hiring a divorce attorney.* Your attorney is a key player on your divorce team and will help you plot a course towards a successful divorce settlement agreement.

CHAPTER 20

EIGHT PLACES HUSBANDS HIDE ASSETS

Mary and John filed for divorce. John was an orthopedic surgeon, and the couple had many assets. Mary was certain that some of John's patients were paying him in cash and that John was not reporting that cash income. So, she decided to put her theory to the test.

Mary's friend, Julie, made an appointment with John and complained of various aches and pains. John gave Julie some basic treatment, and Julie paid in cash. Mary noted the date and amount of the payment . . . and waited.

A few months later, John was ordered by the court to provide cash receipts journals for his medical practice. (A cash receipts journal theoretically lists all payments received via cash, credit card, and check.) To Mary's satisfaction, Julie's cash payment to John did not appear in the cash receipts journal. She now had a bona fide witness who could testify that John was not reporting all of his income. John settled soon afterwards—he did not want to have that particular information presented to the court or to the IRS.[8]

No woman wants to believe that her husband is capable of something as sneaky, unethical, and illegal as hiding assets. But the truth is, these kinds of dirty tricks happen much more frequently than you might expect.

Think about it. Many couples today have complex financial portfolios; and even in the best of times, it can be extremely difficult to keep track of all these moving parts. When a couple decides to divorce, maintaining an accurate accounting of marital assets can get exponentially more complicated, especially if one person has not been very involved in the details of the family's finances and investments. Unfortunately, spouses sometimes try to take advantage of the situation by hiding income and/or assets. Doing so is not overly difficult if they own a business or professional practice.

How can you tell if your spouse is hiding assets? Are there steps can you take to help ensure you have an accurate accounting of your family finances?

For starters, be on the lookout for certain tell-tale signs that your husband has some dirty tricks up his sleeve. For instance, is he starting to act defensively? A husband who suddenly becomes secretive, controlling, or defensive about money could be

---

8 Kohn, M. (2012). *How they stash the cash*, p. 5. San Clemente, CA: Sourced Media Books.

someone who is diverting or dissipating marital assets. Are bank statements and other financial documents no longer being delivered to your home? A change in regular delivery could signal that he's trying to keep you in the dark about diverted or dissipated funds.

In addition to these tell-tale behaviors, you also need to be fully aware of the most common unethical tactics husbands use. If your husband wants to undervalue or disguise/hide marital assets, he may:

1. Purchase items that could easily be overlooked or undervalued. Maybe no one will notice that expensive antique or painting that's now at his office? Were you wondering why he recently made several significant additions to his coin/stamp/art collection?

2. Stash money in a safe deposit box somewhere in the house or elsewhere. Think through your husband's recent habits and activities. Does anything lead you to believe he is hiding assets in actual cash?

3. Underreport income on tax returns and/or financial statements. If it's not reported, it can't be used in a financial analysis.

4. Overpay the IRS or creditors. If your husband overpays, he can get the refund later, after the divorce is final.

5. Defer salary, delay signing new contracts, and/or hold commissions or bonuses. This sneaky trick means this income won't be "on the books" during the divorce proceedings.

6. Create phony debt. Your husband can collude with family members and/or friends to establish phony loans or expenses. Then, he can make payments to the family members or friends, knowing that he'll get all the money back after the divorce is final.

7. Set up a custodial account in the name of a child, using the child's Social Security number. He could also use his girlfriend's Social Security number, in which case it might be difficult to locate the account.

8. Transfer stock. Your husband may transfer stock/investment accounts into the name of family members, business partners, or dummy companies. After the divorce is final, the assets can be transferred back to him.

The list goes on and on . . . and it certainly begs the question: Why would a husband do any of these things? Of course, there are many possible reasons. He may fear not having enough money after the divorce. He may feel he's getting revenge for an infidelity. Maybe he's just greedy and feels that he deserves it! Whatever the reason, hiding assets, income, and debt is not only unethical—it's also illegal and subject to severe penalties if discovered.

Reminder: Make sure to work with a qualified divorce team to help ensure that you have the professional expertise and support required to receive a fair settlement. If you believe your husband has financial dirty tricks up his sleeve, start organizing your personal finances and important documents under the guidance of one of our Divorce Financial Strategists™.

Hot Tip: A lifestyle analysis can serve as an invaluable tool to help determine if your husband is hiding assets and/or income. Conducted by your divorce financial planner, a lifestyle analysis lists all your marital living expenses and connects these expenses to all known sources of income, assets, and loans. Often used to help determine alimony and the division of assets, this analysis also makes it fairly easy to see if and where there is a mismatch. Any discrepancies detected can be tell-tale signs of concealed income and/or assets.

Legal Matters: Hiding assets is unethical and illegal, but, even so, the burden of proof is often on the spouse with fewer financial resources (typically the woman) to prove any such unscrupulous behavior. That's why women must play it smart. They must become knowledgeable and keep their eyes wide open. Ideally, they should be financially aware and consistently involved from the onset of their marriage.

Legal Matters: No matter how tempting it may be, don't snoop. Scrolling through your husband's private emails, listening to his calls or voicemails, or anything of that nature can land you in serious legal trouble too. You'll need to consult with your divorce attorney to understand precisely what type of "investigating" is—and is not—permissible under the laws in your state.

CHAPTER 21

AUTOMATIC TEMPORARY RESTRAINING ORDERS

M ost women are familiar with the words "restraining order" as they apply to circumstances involving physical violence, where one person needs a court order to be protected from the dangerous, aggressive actions of someone else.

However, very few are aware of Automatic Temporary Restraining Orders (called "ATROs," for short) and the role they play in divorce. Let me answer a few fundamental questions about ATROs, while adding insights from a handful of the nation's leading divorce attorneys.

What is an Automatic Temporary Restraining Order?

First things first: ATROs have nothing to do with violence. In fact, they are often considered legal niceties, because they help to ensure a measure of respect between divorcing spouses and establish specific ground rules, so to speak, regarding a couple's assets, insurance policies, beneficiary designations (including wills), etc.

Here's how it works. When a divorce action (or a legal separation, nullity, or paternity action) is filed and then served, it may include an ATRO. In general terms, ATROs are mutual court orders that prohibit either spouse from the following:

1. Selling, transferring, or borrowing against property.

2. Borrowing or selling insurance held for the other spouse.

3. Modifying beneficiaries on policies (health insurance, life insurance, retirement accounts, wills, etc.).

4. Changing bank accounts.

5. Destroying or hiding assets.

In other words, an ATRO prevents either party from changing the financial status quo of the marriage once a divorce action begins.

As Laura A. Wasser, Partner in the family law firm of Wasser, Cooperman, and Carter (Los Angeles) explained to me, a "freeze on assets" can be critical, particularly if one party controls the family finances: "ATROs are helpful to family law attorneys, as they establish a broad freeze on assets that might otherwise be under only one party's control or discretion. They help to level the playing field. In addition to the prophylactic function, ATROs can keep costs down by providing forensic accountants with a snapshot of the financial picture. Too much post-separation movement during the pendency of the action is potentially confusing for accountants and attorneys who are trying to assess the estate."[9] In a nutshell, ATROs freeze your finances, so they can be evaluated accurately.

Often, these orders are a separate document attached to the Summons of a Petition for Dissolution, but not always. In California, ATROs are summarized on the back of the Summons of a Petition for Dissolution. They become immediately effective upon the plaintiff when he or she files the action and upon the defendant upon the service of a summons. They remain in effect until the final judgment is signed by the court.

Since an ATRO is "automatic," will it be automatically included in my divorce petition?

Not always. Despite the word "automatic" in the title, only some states include ATROs in every divorce petition. If you live in a state that does not require ATROs, your attorney will have to request one from

---

9 Wasser, L. (2012). Personal communication.

the court. Also, don't assume that your accounts and policies will automatically be notified that an ATRO is in effect. For instance, in states where an ATRO prohibits the modification of beneficiaries, you would need to inform your bank, stock brokerage, and insurance companies about the divorce action. The courts do not do this!

What happens if my husband violates the terms of the ATRO?

ATROs are legal documents designed to protect both parties. Violation of the ATRO terms by either spouse can lead to serious legal consequences.

Can terms of the ATRO be altered as the divorce action proceeds?

Yes. If both spouses agree to the terms, the court can issue a modification of the ATRO.

Are there elements of my financial portfolio not included in an ATRO?

Yes. Again, speaking in general terms, the following are usually not considered violations of an ATRO:

- ➡ Payment of attorney fees. You are allowed to use your assets to retain legal counsel.

- ➡ Spending assets in the "usual course of business." Of course, the courts will need to make assessments as to the nature of the business and whether or not the dissipation of assets is "usual."

Attorney Wasser, whose client list includes Maria Shriver, Heidi Klum, Angelina Jolie, Christina Aguilera, Mariah Carey, Britney Spears, and many others, has seen the courts exercise broad discretion in this area. She explained to me, "Also to be considered is the gifting aspect which ATROs may preclude. While paying for an aged parent's monthly nursing home bills may fall under the usual course of business umbrella, annual gifts to adult children may not," she said. "Courts have broad discretion in this area. I had one client who was quite perplexed to learn that the ATROs would keep him from paying his girlfriend's very high credit card bills once the Petition had been filed and served."

As always, check with your divorce attorney regarding the details of your particular case.

Do ATRO requirements vary from state to state?

Yes. As with many aspects of divorce, different states handle ATROs differently—and not all states have them. "The automatic TRO is not something that is universally implemented across the country and doesn't apply to New Jersey," Bari Weinberger, Managing Partner at Weinberger Law Group (New Jersey), told me. "In New Jersey, all orders must be done by consent or on notice with an opportunity for both sides to be heard. An exception to this rule exists when there is an Order to Show Cause with temporary restraints. But even in this circumstance, the court has a hearing before it can become final."[10]

ATROs aren't routine in South Carolina, either: "In South Carolina, ATROS are not automatic, although it has been proposed. Therefore, parties often have to go to the unnecessary expense of filing for an ex parte (emergency) order, where there is a fear that a party will be damaged by the actions of another party before a temporary hearing," Marie-Louise Ramsdale, Owner of the Ramsdale Law Firm in Charleston, SC, explained. "For example, I have had to file for an emergency ex parte order requiring a spouse to keep his ill spouse on the health insurance policy when he threatened to remove her."[11]

Even in New York, ATROs are relatively new. In 2009, the New York State legislature passed a law that prohibits either spouse from hiding or liquidating assets once a divorce action has commenced.[12] This new law is generally hailed as a benefit to the non-monied spouse (typically, but not always, the woman), because it provides her with a level of certainty and eliminates the time and money required to obtain an injunction from the courts.

---

10 Weinberger, B. (2012). Personal communication.

11 Ramsdale, M. (2012). Personal communication.

12 The details of this law are available at http://www.courts.state. ny.us/rules/trialcourts/236.pdf.

"Prior to the institution of the automatic orders in matrimonial proceedings, the burden would be put on the party who feared that there might be a transfer, dissipation, or a change in the assets to apply to the court to seek a restraint. It was much more costly, as a motion had to be made, and there was always the lingering concern about whether such steps were necessary in any given matter," Judith L. Poller, Partner at Pryor Cashman (New York City), explained to me. "The ATROs now shift the burden to the parties from the beginning of the proceedings to ensure that a status quo remains in place. Notwithstanding these new orders, however, it is still necessary to continue to monitor the assets to ensure that, in fact, nothing is changing. Unfortunately, people do not always abide by the law, and it is often necessary to remind both parties that they are limited in what they can do during the proceedings. There is very little law on the consequences of a violation of the ATROs, but the threat of bringing a contempt proceeding does have some teeth."[13]

At first, all the details and finer points of ATROs may seem a bit perplexing. However, a qualified divorce team will make sure all the different moving parts come together to form a successful strategy.

Your attorney will file the divorce action and the ATRO according to the regulations in your state. Then, once your financial status quo is "frozen," a

---

13 Poller, J. (2012). Personal communication.

Certified Divorce Financial Analyst, like the Divorce Financial Strategists™ at Bedrock Divorce Advisors, can analyze your financial situation and chart a course with your attorney for a successful settlement and a sound, stable financial future.

Reminder: An Automatic Temporary Restraining Order (ATRO) is a court order that prevents either party from changing the financial status quo of the marriage once a divorce action begins.

Hot Tip: It is not unusual for spouses to begin hiding assets and/or income once divorce is anticipated. As always, your best defense will be a good offense, so stay an active participant in your family finances throughout the marriage. At the very least, you need to know the basics about your major assets, income, investments, bills, and debts. If you are contemplating divorce, start organizing your personal finances and important documents under the guidance of a qualified divorce financial planner.

Legal Matters: ATROs are not "automatic" in every state, so be sure to consult with your attorney to learn the specific steps your state requires for you to freeze the financial status quo of your marriage. Once neither party can change the marital financial portfolio, your assets can be fully and accurately assessed.

CHAPTER 22

HOW TO DIVORCE-PROOF YOUR BUSINESS

If you're a business owner, your business is probably the most valuable financial asset you possess. Undoubtedly, you've spent countless hours and precious resources nurturing and growing it. But, have you ever thought about what would happen to your business if you and your husband were to divorce?

As remarkable as it sounds, under certain circumstances, your spouse could be entitled to as much as 50 percent of your business. Are you comfortable with that scenario? Since it's probably safe to assume you will not want your ex-husband to become your business partner, let's take a look at steps you can take to protect your business in the event of a divorce.

The Fundamentals

First, you need to be familiar with the ground rules. For instance, you'll need to determine if your business qualifies as separate property or marital property. And then you'll need to consider these nuances, as well:

➻ In many states, if your separately owned property increases in value during the marriage, that increase is considered marital property.

➻ If the increase is considered marital property, some states will make a distinction between an increase resulting from active appreciation and an increase resulting from passive appreciation.

Active vs. Passive Appreciation

A good understanding of active and passive appreciation can help you divorce-proof your business. As discussed in chapter 12, **active appreciation** is appreciation due in part to the direct or indirect contributions or efforts of the other spouse (e.g., your husband helped you grow your business by giving you ideas and advice; he entertained clients with you; he helped raise the kids and did household chores, which allowed you to work late, entertain clients, travel to conventions, etc.).

Passive appreciation is appreciation due to outside forces, such as supply and demand and inflation (e.g., a parcel of land increases in value even though you and your husband made no improvements to it). However, if you used marital income and/or assets to pay the mortgage and/or taxes on this parcel of land, your husband might have a very good argument that this property, or at least the increase in value during your marriage, should now be considered marital property. (As you can see, this can get quite complicated and convoluted.)

On top of all this, there are other state laws which determine how your marital property is divided, so you'll also need to know if you live in a community property state or an equitable distribution state (see chapter 8 for a review of these terms).

Prenups and Asset Protection Trusts

One excellent way to divorce-proof your business is to have it protected in a prenuptial agreement. Since I discuss prenups in detail in the next chapter (see chapter 23), I won't belabor the point here. In a nutshell, a prenup is a contract signed by both parties before their wedding. It specifies what each spouse's property rights and expectations (including alimony) would be upon divorce. A well-drafted prenup can override both community property and equitable distribution state laws, and the courts will usually respect such agreements (which is one reason they are so powerful).

If you are concerned that the terms of your pre-nup could be challenged and possibly not upheld in the future, or if your fiancé refuses to sign a prenup, or if you don't even want to ask, then you should definitely consider protecting your business by establishing a Domestic or Foreign Asset Protection Trust.

In essence, this consists of transferring the ownership of your separate property, including your company, into this trust. (This works for most entities, such as C Corporations, Limited Liability Companies, Limited Partnerships—but not necessarily for S Corporations. Only certain types of trusts can own S Corporation stock, so if your company is an S Corporation, please discuss your options with a trust attorney who is experienced with asset protection trusts.)

Without going into further detail about the various types of trusts and how they work, suffice it to say that using a trust could make the entire issue of separate property appreciation a moot point. How? Because once you have established a trust, the trust (and not you) legally owns your separate property, including your company.

It's important to note that the transfer of your separate property into the trust *does not* require any approval from your fiancé, but it should be done while you are still single. Also, the use of this trust would certainly not preclude you from also having a prenup. However, the prenup might no longer need to address the issue of your separate property and its appreciation. Instead, it could focus on how marital property (and possibly his separate property) would be divided and who would receive alimony, in what amount, and for how long.

Postnups

A postnup (short for "postnuptial agreement") is a contract similar to a prenup, except it is entered into and signed after the wedding. A postnup can help to protect your business; but, if you're considering one, please proceed with caution. Several states still don't recognize postnups; and even when they do, postnups are challenged and invalidated much more frequently than prenups.

Before marriage, the parties are entering into an agreement much like two business people entering into a contract, and neither party has any legal family law rights on the other. Theoretically, either party can walk away. However after marriage, the situation is very different. The married couple now has very well-defined legal rights regarding support and property division, and both husband and wife are considered to be in a fiduciary relationship with each other (meaning each party has to act in the best interests of the other party). When negotiating a postnup, however, one party will typically be giving up some of those rights; therefore, any transactions between them will be viewed with caution. Postnups are usually held to a higher standard of fairness than prenups on the theory that individuals have less bargaining power once married.

Nevertheless, I still believe postnups can offer your business a measure of protection. If you don't have a prenup, try to get a postnup. It's better than nothing, provided you understand that a postnup is not nearly as ironclad as a prenup.

Buy-Sell Agreements

Almost every business with two or more owners should have a buy-sell agreement in place. If you don't have one, you need to get this taken care of as soon as possible. A well-drafted buy-sell agreement will determine exactly how, and under what terms and conditions, the transfer of an ownership interest in the business will occur—if and when there are certain triggering events, such as death, disability, departure, or (for our purposes) divorce. In particular, buy-sell agreements can prevent ex-spouses of any of your business partners from gaining ownership of the business.

Since the ownership interests in a closely held business are fairly illiquid, a well-drafted buy-sell agreement should provide for the following:

- A market for the sale and/or purchase of those ownership interests;

- A mechanism to determine the price, terms, and conditions for the sale and/or purchase of those ownership interests; and

- The source of funds for the purchase of any ownership interests (life or disability insurance, a sinking fund, cash on hand, line-of-credit or a loan, a combination thereof, etc.).

In addition, a buy-sell agreement can (and often should) do the following:

- Prohibit an owner (or his/her estate) from transferring and/or selling any ownership interests to third parties without the prior written consent of the other owners;

- Restrict the ownership of any interest in the business to an existing group;

- Automatically convert the ownership interest into a non-voting interest upon a triggering event;

- Provide the business and/or other owners with the mandatory right or right of first refusal to buy the ownership interests from any departing owner, the estate of a deceased owner, or the ex-spouse of a current or departed owner; and

- Require all owners to have an acceptable prenuptial agreement in place before marriage or remarriage that would require that owner's soon-to-be spouse to waive any and all rights to any ownership interest in the business in the event of a future divorce.

Operating Agreement/Partnership Agreement/Shareholder Agreement

The purpose of an Operating Agreement, Partnership Agreement, and Shareholder Agreement is to formalize the understanding between you and the other owners as to how the business will be owned and managed. In general, Operating Agreements are used with Limited Liability Companies; Partnership Agreements are used with Partnerships, including Limited Partnerships; and Shareholder Agreements are used for C and S Corporations.

Even though it is not a legal requirement for your business to have such an agreement, it certainly makes good business sense to do so. Without having some type of operating agreement in place, your business might be forced to operate in accordance with your home state's default operating requirements. Wouldn't you rather manage and operate your business the way you want to, instead of the way your state has decided it should be run?

In addition, a well-drafted agreement will stipulate what is expected of each owner; how profits and losses are assigned; procedures for transferring, buying, and/or selling ownership interests; and just about anything else you want it to say, including restrictions on the ability of ex-spouses of owners to have any ownership interests whatsoever in the business.

In most cases, the buy-sell language is either included in the operating/partnership/shareholders' agreement, or it is contained in a separate buy-sell agreement.

Paying Off Your Ex-Husband

In the absence of a prenup or postnup agreement, all or part of your business will probably be considered marital property, unless you were able to transfer your ownership of the business into a Domestic or Foreign Asset Protection Trust while you were still single.

Beyond that, if your husband is or was employed by you or your company, helped run the company in any way, or even contributed business ideas and advice during your marriage, then he may very well be entitled to a substantial percentage of your business. Naturally, the greater his involvement in your business, the bigger that percentage will be. (If your business has other owners in addition to you, then your husband would own a percentage of your share.)

If, for whatever reason, your husband is entitled to an ownership interest in your business, and you don't want to be partners after the divorce, you have a number of ways to pay him off, including:

➻ Using your share of other marital assets, including cash, stocks, real estate, retirement funds, etc.

➻ Establishing a Property Settlement Note, which is a long-term payout with interest of the amount you owe your ex-spouse for the value of his share of your business.

➻ Creating an ESOP (Employee Stock Ownership Plan) to raise funds by selling a portion of your business to your employees.

An ESOP is a tax-advantaged, qualified employee retirement plan. An ESOP is similar to a stock bonus plan, except it is designed to provide your employees with an ownership interest in your business.

In essence, you are selling a minority interest in your business to your employees. With an ESOP in place, you have a ready-made marketplace for the sale of your otherwise illiquid business ownership interests. In addition, many studies have shown that employees who are part owners of the business they work for are better employees, because they now operate with an owner's mentality.

Reminder: To be truly effective, these protective methods should be in place well before the possibility of divorce enters anyone's mind. Obviously, something like a prenup needs to be signed before the wedding, but techniques such as transfers to an irrevocable trust need to be done years in advance. Depending on your state's fraudulent transfer laws, transactions can be voided up to seven years after the transfer!

Hot Tip: If you have children, you may want to start thinking about your estate-planning goals in the context of protecting your business ownership interests (and any other assets) from a possible future divorce.

If you start gifting some of your ownership interests in your business (or any other assets) into a Discretionary Spendthrift Trust set up for the benefit of your children, not only have you protected those ownership interests from your own possible future divorce (since you no longer legally own those interests), but you have also protected those ownership interests from your children's possible future divorce. That's because once assets are in a Discretionary Spendthrift Trust, a trustee will control them. You and your children will no longer have any control over those assets. Therefore, no one can get at the trust's assets, including a divorcing spouse or creditor.

Legal Matters: For our purposes, once the possibility of a divorce is actually on the horizon, any transfer, gift, or sale of assets (business or personal) that removes those assets from the reach of your future ex-spouse, or makes it difficult for him to access those assets, could be deemed a fraudulent transfer.

That would also include those instances where you might sell or gift an asset for an amount far less than what it's worth. For example, if you sell your house to your brother for $100, that would also be considered a fraudulent transfer.

In most states, the "look-back" period for fraudulent transfers ranges from four to seven years. So, for example, if you transferred, gifted, or sold an asset for less than its value three years ago, and now you and your husband are getting a divorce, that transfer, gift, or sale could be deemed a fraudulent transfer, and a judge could void it, making that asset available for distribution in your divorce. The same would hold true even if at the time of that transfer, gift, or sale you and your husband were still happily married and neither one of you had any thoughts of divorce.

That's why it is absolutely imperative for you to start divorce-proofing your business as soon as possible.

CHAPTER 23

PRENUPS AND POSTNUPS

In 1985, Steven Spielberg and Amy Irving wrote a prenuptial agreement on a cocktail napkin. Four years later, Amy contested the agreement—and won. As a result, she received a settlement of about $100 million, or half of her ex-husband's earnings, after just four years of marriage. The reason? Her attorney wasn't present, allowing her to contest the prenup on the grounds of fairness, full disclosure, and duress.[14]

If you think prenups are only for older, affluent, and/or celebrity couples, think again. Prenups are becoming increasingly common—especially now that many people enter marriage at a later age with significant assets, such as cars, 401(k)s, real estate, businesses, etc. Long considered stuffy, stodgy, and

---

14 Todorova, A. (2006). When prenups fail. *Smart Money*, December 7. Retrieved August 1, 2012, from http://www.smartmoney.com/spend/family-money/when-prenups-fail-20471/

decidedly unromantic, the prenup is beginning to win favor as a reasonable, practical, and smart sign of trust between a woman and her fiancé.

So, before you dismiss the possibility, let's review the basics to help you decide if a prenup is right for you.

A prenup can help protect your property rights and financial interests.

A prenup (short for "prenuptial agreement") is a contract signed by both parties before their wedding. By using a prenup, both the husband-to-be and the wife-to-be can decide certain financial issues in advance. For example, a prenup can specify the following:

- What property will be considered separate property,
- What property will be considered marital property,
- How any marital property should be divided,
- Particulars about estate planning and inheritances, and even
- How much alimony will be paid, and for how long, if there's a break-up down the road.

In short, the prenup details what the couple's property rights and expectations would be upon divorce. If done correctly, a prenup can be an excellent way to supersede your state's marital laws; however, in order for it to be "done correctly," both the husband-to-be and the wife-to-be must be represented by separate attorneys. In addition, the agreement:

- Must be in writing.
- Must provide full disclosure (no hiding of assets and/or liabilities).
- Must be executed voluntarily and without coercion.
- Must be executed by both parties, preferably in front of witnesses.
- Cannot be unconscionable, meaning that it cannot be completely lopsided, giving one party much more than the other.
- Should be in a recordable format.

And of course, just to reiterate, the prenup must be executed *before* the wedding!

Many women find even the idea of a prenup awkward and unromantic. That's unfortunate. In reality, a prenup underscores a couple's mature level of commitment and trust. Since the agreement requires full disclosure about personal assets and candid discussions about potential financial concerns, a prenup can actually serve to bring a couple closer together. With a prenup in place, the marriage can begin on a firm foundation with clear and consensual expectations.

Of course, a prenup is not the only way a bride-to-be can protect her property rights and financial interests before the wedding. For instance, she can establish a Domestic or Foreign Asset Protection Trust or pursue other options that do not require a fiancé's approval.

A postnup is a contract established while you're married.

If you're already married and missed out on the opportunity to establish a prenup before your wedding, or your financial situation has dramatically changed, or you feel there's reason to modify a prenup already in place, you may want to consider creating a postnup. Similar to a prenup, a postnup (short for "postnuptial agreement") is a contract between husband and wife, but it is entered into and signed *after* the wedding.

There are many reasons that you may want to protect your assets with a postnup. Maybe you're establishing a new business in your name or working to patent an invention. Perhaps you're writing the next bestselling book or agreed to quit your job to take care of the kids. If there's any chance your financial situation may change (for better or worse), you may want to establish your property rights and the expectations surrounding any shift in finances.

When celebrities divorce, one of the biggest points of contention is typically intellectual property rights. These rights cover property such as patents, trademarks, copyrights and royalties, and other contractual rights. Depending on the individual circumstances, they can be worth thousands, if not millions, of dollars.

What's more, any intellectual property rights obtained during a marriage may be considered marital property—and that means they may be divided during divorce. Although the specific rules vary from state to state, the general rule of thumb governing intellectual and other property is this: **Value that's created during the marriage must be divided.**

Despite all the potential benefits, postnups come with possible pitfalls, as well. For instance, a number of states don't recognize postnuptial agreements; and even in the states that do, they are frequently challenged and often invalidated. Still, if you're a married woman involved in a business endeavor or career that makes you (or has the potential to make you) much wealthier than your husband, my advice is simple: Having a postnup in place is usually better than having nothing at all.

 Reminder: You may want to consider a pren-up if you:

↦ Have considerable assets such as a home, real estate investments, stock (including stock options), or retirement funds that make you (or have the potential to make you) much wealthier than your fiancé;

- ➻ Own all or part of a business or professional practice;
- ➻ Have children and/or grandchildren;
- ➻ Have loved ones, such as elderly parents, who need care;
- ➻ Are expecting an inheritance; or
- ➻ Have (or are pursuing) a degree or license in a potentially lucrative profession.

Hot Tip: To be truly effective, any protective methods I discussed above should be in place long before divorce is a possibility. Obviously, something like a prenuptial agreement needs to be signed before you are married, but even techniques such as transfers to an irrevocable trust need to be done *years* in advance. Depending on your state's fraudulent transfer laws, transactions can be voided up to seven years after the transfer.

Legal Matters: If you're a business owner looking to protect your business interests before you get married, consider a Domestic or Foreign Asset Protection Trust. A financial vehicle like this transfers the ownership of your separate property (including your company) into the trust, and it can work for most entities. This includes C Corporations, Limited Liability Companies, and Limited Partnerships—but not necessarily S Corporations.

Only certain types of trusts can own S Corporation stock, so this is something that you would need to discuss with a trust attorney who is experienced with asset protection trusts.

How these types of trusts work is somewhat complicated, but the bottom line is that by creating the right type of trust, you can make the entire issue of separate vs. marital property irrelevant. That's because the trust, rather than you, would legally own your separate property, including your company.

CHAPTER 24

MOVING FORWARD: SEVEN STEPS FOR FINANCIAL STABILITY POST-DIVORCE

Remember that divorce emotional rollercoaster I described in the introduction to this book—the wild ride that left you feeling "up" one minute and "down" the next?

Well, here's something else you must know: Over time, as your divorce progresses and you gain some control over your personal finances, your emotions will begin to stabilize, and you'll be able to set your sights firmly on a bright, new future as a single woman.

Clearly, your life will be different. But adapting to and even embracing these changes will help to ensure your success. For example, as a single woman, you will now be fully in control of your financial portfolio. You will have to keep a careful eye on your income, expenses, and debt, if you have any. You'll have to pay your bills, save and invest for your retirement, plan for college if you have children, map out other long-term goals, and plan for the savings and investments you will need to help you achieve it all.

Naturally that list of responsibilities may seem a bit daunting at first (particularly if you weren't very involved with the family finances while you were married), but I assure you: *You can do it!* Take it step by step, learning as you go, and it's likely you will find, as most women do, that it's empowering to make financial decisions and to be the one who's in control of your financial portfolio. Of course, working with a financial advisor who has the experience and training to specifically help divorced women accomplish their goals and objectives can be extremely helpful. Careful and conservative investments coupled with living within your means are the keys to making your divorce settlement last as long as it possibly can.

What can you do to stay on the best path forward? Here are a few key steps to get you started towards financial stability post-divorce. Once your divorce settlement agreement is finalized, you will need to take the following six steps.

1. Update accounts. Even though it may sound mundane, this financial housekeeping step is absolutely essential. If you changed your name as a result of the divorce, you'll need to get a new Social Security Card, driver's license, passport, and credit card(s). You'll also need to notify your utilities, insurance, and credit card companies, the bank, the motor vehicle department, and your children's school(s) about any change of name and/ or address. The titles on all assets, such as cars and houses, will have to be modified and recorded with mortgage companies—and it's likely you'll want to update beneficiaries on your life insurance, 401(k), pensions, and IRA accounts, as well.

See the checklist below for an overview of many of the accounts and policies typically needing prompt attention post-divorce.

2. Develop a comprehensive financial plan. If you had a Lifestyle Analysis prepared during your divorce, you should have a very clear understanding of what funds came into the marriage (income) and what funds went out (expenses). Use this as a basis for developing a budget going forward. Of course, you'll need to keep tabs on financial matters in the short-term. (What are your day-to-day expenses? How much are monthly utilities, the mortgage, car payments, etc.?) You'll need to establish a plan for the long-term, as well. (Who is going to pay for college tuition? What do you need to save for retirement?) If your divorce settlement agreement included any lump-sum payments (for alimony, pension rollovers, sale of a vacation home, etc.), you'll also need to develop a sound strategy for management of these assets. Establishing and then sticking to a financial plan is essential for financial stability and peace of mind.

3. Build your credit. Good credit forms the foundation of your financial portfolio and will help you secure loans in your name in the future. The first step in building good credit is to get a copy of your credit report. (AnnualCreditReport.com offers them for free.) Your current credit score is the starting point for your future, so make sure you address any inaccuracies in the report. If you are employed and/or already have credit cards in your name, the process of building your credit will be relatively straightforward. Use your credit cards regularly, and pay off the balance on time each month—and you'll watch your credit score rise.

4. Seek help from an experienced financial advisor. More specifically, look for a financial advisor who is trained and experienced in working with women post-divorce.

All of the fundamental components of a sound financial plan—creating a budget, investing, planning for retirement, making sure you don't outlive your money, understanding your goals and aspirations (travel, leave money to children, grandchildren, and/or charity, etc.), saving for college, life insurance, and so forth—should be completed under the guidance of an investment professional/advisor who is very familiar with the needs and issues of divorced women. For example, just as women all over the country depend on Bedrock Divorce Advisors to help them before and during their divorce, many of these same women (and others) rely on our sister company, Bedrock Wealth Management, LLC, post-divorce to help them make their divorce settlements last as long as possible.

Using our many years of experience and specialized training, we assist with a wide range of financial concerns, including:

- Budgeting
- Retirement planning
- Asset protection and insurance
- Estate planning
- Investments
- College savings
- and much more.

5. Add other experienced professionals to your post-divorce team, as well. In addition to an experienced financial planner, I believe most women post-divorce can benefit from the assistance of the following:

- **An estate-planning attorney.** This type of lawyer will work in conjunction with your financial advisor to help you with your estate planning needs and the legal issues concerning your will, medical directives, trusts, charitable giving, etc.

- **A therapist or counselor.** A compassionate therapist will help you cope with the emotional challenges associated with starting your life as a single woman.

- **A vocational counselor.** Need some tips for re-entering the job market? Or, perhaps you want to start your own business? A vocational counselor can provide the guidance and know-how so you make these transitions successfully.

6. Make sure you've completed everything on this post-divorce "To Do" list:

1. Obtain a copy of your certified divorce decree. Make extra copies, and store them in a secure location.

2. Close any joint credit accounts.

3. Remove your husband's name and/or change your name/address on all remaining accounts, such as:

   ⟶ Bank, brokerage, and investment accounts
   ⟶ Credit cards
   ⟶ Driver's license, automobile title, registration, and insurance policies
   ⟶ Employers' records
   ⟶ IRS records
   ⟶ Life, health, homeowner's, and disability insurance policies
   ⟶ Post office
   ⟶ Professional licenses
   ⟶ Social Security card
   ⟶ Title to real property
   ⟶ Utility bills

4. Research your health insurance options and apply for COBRA, if necessary.

5. If your divorce decree requires

→ A Qualified Domestic Relations Order (QDRO): Provide the QDRO to appropriate banks, brokerages, pension plan advisor, 401(k) administrators, etc. (Even better, have this step completed before your divorce is finalized.)

→ A quitclaim or warranty deed: Make certain the appropriate documents are executed and recorded.

→ The transfer of title to property (automobiles, boats, etc.): Complete the transfer by signing and delivering the necessary documents.

6. Open a new bank account. Consider establishing direct deposit or income withholding for child support, spousal support, and/or alimony payments.

7. Open a new credit card account and request a copy of your credit report.

8. Disinherit your husband. Write and execute new wills, trusts, medical directives, and/or living wills and powers of attorney. Don't forget to change the beneficiaries on your life insurance, 401(k), pension, and IRA accounts.

9. Establish a system to keep track of all child support made/received, alimony payments made/received, medical expenses, etc.

Enjoy your new life. Once you complete the previous six steps, you will be well on your way to establishing a secure financial foundation for your future. After all, nothing nurtures self-confidence like firm footing and a solid plan—one that offers you positive reinforcement every step along the way. You'll learn to stick with a budget, strengthen your credit score, and manage your assets. Then, you'll be able to set new goals and achieve even more.

Reminder: The financial needs of a divorced woman are very different from those of a married couple, and I advise you to work with a financial advisor who completely understands those differences. The fundamental components of your post-divorce financial plan should be completed under the guidance of an investment professional/advisor who is familiar with the needs and issues of divorced women.

Hot Tip: Any woman who is not employed and/or doesn't already have a credit history in her name is likely to face challenges establishing good credit. New federal regulations are making it more difficult than ever for women with little or no income to establish credit on their own, so prepare yourself for the possibility that securing credit could be somewhat time-consuming and is likely to require more than simply filling out an application or making a single phone call.

Legal Matters: Continue working with your divorce attorney until the QDRO is properly filed with all appropriate entities, property titles are transferred, etc. Don't forget to change your will, trusts, medical directives, and/or living wills and powers of attorney, as well.

CHAPTER 25

BONUS CHAPTERS

You've now finished reading, Divorce: Think Financially, Not Emotionally®, which means you've taken the first step in getting the financial information you need to come through your divorce with the necessary resources to live comfortably, taking care of yourself and your children.

So what's next?

What if you could continue to receive BONUS CHAPTERS – for FREE?

Well you can!

Just go to http://thinkfinancially.com/bonuschapters/ and you'll be able to receive free, immediate access to all my bonus chapters from Divorce: Think Financially, Not Emotionally®.

CHAPTER 26

WANT MORE?

Schedule a 60-Minute In-Depth, One-on-One Consultation with Jeff Landers

After reading Divorce: Think Financially, Not Emotionally®, you may have questions specific to your particular situation.

Don't worry. Jeff Landers can answer those questions, too. He offers personal, hour-long consultations to help women like you who are tackling the financial complexities of divorce.

Best of all, Jeff is available at your convenience, regardless of where you live. Your one-on-one consultation can take place over the telephone or in-person in Manhattan –whichever you prefer.

Just visit http://www.bedrockdivorce.com/contact. php to schedule an appointment.

Upon receipt of your request, Jeff will email you a detailed questionnaire for you to complete and return before your consultation. The answers you provide will give Jeff the background information necessary for him to optimize the time he spends with you.

APPENDIX A

DIVORCE FINANCIAL CHECKLIST

The following is a checklist of the financial information that you will need:

1. Income Tax Returns. Completed personal, corporate, partnership, joint venture, or other income tax returns (federal, state and local), including W-2, 1099, and K-1 forms, in your possession or control for the last 5 years, including all amended tax returns. Do you expect any tax refunds?

   1A Business Financial Statements. Net worth statement—balance sheet or list of assets and liabilities Income statement—cash flow or income and expense statement.

2. Income Information. Current income information, including payroll stubs and all other evidence of income (investment property, rental/lease agreements, dividends, interest, royalties, lottery winnings, etc.) since the filing of your last tax return.

3. Personal Property Tax Returns filed in this state or anywhere else from the start of the marriage. ☐

4. Banking Information. All monthly bank statements, passbooks, check registers, deposit slips, cancelled checks, and bank charge notices on personal and business accounts, certificates of deposit, and money market and retirement accounts from banks, savings and loan institutions, credit unions, or other institutions in which you or your spouse has an interest. ☐

5. Financial Statements submitted to banks, lending institutions, or any other persons or entities, which were prepared by you or your spouse at any time during the last five (5) years. ☐

6. Loan Applications made within the last five (5) years. ☐

7. Brokerage Statements. Statements from all accounts of securities and/or commodities dealers or mutual funds maintained by you or your spouse during the marriage and held individually, jointly, or as a trustee or guardian. ☐

8. Stocks, Bonds, and Mutual Funds. Certificates, if available, of accounts owned by either spouse during the marriage or pre-owned by you. ☐

9. Stock Options. All records pertaining to stock options held in any corporation or other entity, exercised or not exercised (include any restricted stock). ☐

10. Pension, Money Purchase Plans, Profit Sharing, Employee Stock Option Plans, Deferred Compensation Agreement, and Retirement Plans (401(k), 403(b), 412(e)(3), 457, military, IRA, Roth IRA, SEP-IRA, Keogh) or any other kind of plan owned by you or by any corporation in which you and/or your spouse have been a participant during the marriage, including annual statements. ☐

11. Wills and Trust Agreements (include any Powers of Attorney, etc.) executed by you or in which you have a present or contingent interest or in which you are a beneficiary, trustee, executor, or guardian and from which benefits have been received, are being received, or will be received and which are or were in existence during the past five (5) years, including inter vivos trusts. All records of declaration of trust and minute books for all trusts to which you are a party, including the certificates, if any, showing such interest and copies of all statements, receipts, disbursements, investments, and other transactions. ☐

12. Life Insurance or certificate of life insurance policies now in existence, insuring your life or the life of your spouse, and statements of the cash value, if available. ☐

13. General Insurance. Copies of insurance policies, including but not limited to annuities, health, accident, disability, casualty, motor vehicles of any kind, property liability, including contents, and insurance owned by the parties during the past five (5) years of the marriage. ☐

14. Outstanding Debts. Documents reflecting all debts owed to you or by you (including those cosigned by you), secured or unsecured, including mortgages, personal loans, credit card statements, promissory notes and lawsuits pending or previously filed in any court. ☐

15. Business Records or ledgers in your possession and control that are either personal or business-related, together with all accounts and journals. ☐

16. Real Property. Any deeds of property in which you and/or your spouse have an interest, together with evidence of all contributions, in cash or otherwise, made by you or on your behalf, toward the acquisition of such real estate during the marriage. Include all purchase agreements, mortgages, notes, property tax statements, rental/lease agreements, appraisals and all expenses associated with each property. ☐

16A List of real property owned prior to your marriage as well as real property acquired during the marriage by gift and/or inheritance. ☐

17. Sale and Option Agreements on any real estate owned by you either individually, through another person or entity, jointly, or as trustee or guardian. ☐

18. Personal Property. Documents, invoices, contracts, insurance policies, and appraisals on all personal property, including furniture, fixtures, jewelry, artwork, furnishings, furs, equipment, antiques, and any type of collections (coin, stamps, gold, etc.), owned by you individually, jointly, as trustee or guardian, or through any other person or entity during the term of the marriage. ☐

18A. List of personal property owned prior to your marriage as well as personal property acquired during the marriage by gift and/or inheritance.

19. Motor Vehicles. All financing agreements and titles to all motor vehicles owned by you, individually or jointly, at any time during the last five (5) years, including airplanes, boats, automobiles, or any other types of motor vehicles.

20. Corporate Interests. All records showing any kind of personal interest in any corporation (foreign or domestic) or any other entities not evidenced by certificate or other instrument.

21. Partnership and Joint Venture Agreements to which you have been a party during the marriage.

22. Employment Records during the term of the marriage, showing evidence of wages, salaries, bonuses, commissions, raises, promotions, expense accounts, and other benefits or deductions of any kind whether in cash, stock and/or other property. All records showing any fringe benefits available to you or your spouse from any business entity including without limitation auto, travel, private aircraft, boat, apartment/home, entertainment, country club, health club/spa, educational, vacation pay, severance pay, personal living expenses, etc.

23. Employment contracts under which you or your spouse have performed services during the past five (5) years, including a list of description of any oral contracts.

24. Charge Account statements for the past five (5) years.

25. Membership cards or documents identifying participation rights in any country clubs, health clubs/spas, key clubs, private clubs, associations, or fraternal group organizations during the past five (5) years of the marriage, together with all monthly statements.

26. Judgments and pleadings in which you have been a party to, either as Plaintiff or Defendant, during the marriage, including any Personal Injury Awards.

27. Appraisals of any asset owned by you for the past five (5) years.

28. Safe Deposit Boxes. Include a list of its contents.

29. Mileage/travel awards. Provide statements of all awards both granted and used and any dates of expiration.

30. Anything else that you think may be an asset.

ACKNOWLEDGMENTS

I would like to offer my thanks and gratitude to the following people:

Amy Osmond Cook, Publisher of Sourced Media Books, who took my manuscript and did a fantastic job of turning it into the book you now hold.

Bill Greaves, who did an amazing job with the book cover design.

Kathy Siranosian, who helped me turn my ideas, expertise, and grammatically incorrect writing into a terrific manuscript. I could not have done it without her.

Laura Wasser, Sonja Morgan, and Liz Smith, who were kind enough to read my manuscript and provide me with some great blurbs for this book. I very much appreciate their generosity.

My clients, who inspired me to write this book.

And special thanks to my wife and daughters for their ongoing love and support.

ABOUT THE AUTHOR

Jeffrey A. Landers holds a bachelor's degree in psychology from Columbia University and studied law at Pace University School of Law before joining Wells Fargo Advisors, where he began his divorce practice helping women undergoing financially complex divorces.

Backed by more than three decades of financial experience and an education in law, he went on to earn the Institute for Divorce Financial Analysts' designation as a Certified Divorce Financial Analyst™ (CDFA) and underwent significant additional advanced training in divorce finance before founding Bedrock Divorce Advisors in early 2010.

Jeff writes the weekly "Divorce Dollars and Sense" blog for Forbes.com and has authored multiple articles on divorce for *The Huffington Post, The New York Post, Inc.com,* and others. He has also served on the advisory board of *Enterprising Women,* a magazine devoted to women business owners.

Jeff holds the Chartered Retirement Planning Counselor® (CRPC) designation and is the founder of Bedrock Divorce Advisors' sister firm, Bedrock Wealth Management, LLC, which provides post-divorce retirement planning, asset protection, investment services, insurance, college savings, and more with the goal of making each woman's divorce settlement last as long as possible while helping her achieve her personal goals.

Jeff enjoys running marathons, studying Kung-Fu, and spending time with his wife of 29 years and two daughters.

INDEX

D

E

F

H

INDEX

I

income 19, 21, 25, 27, 31, 33, 36, 42, 50, 56, 61, 68, 88, 101, 102,
        105, 106, 119, 120, 121, 128, 135, 139, 140, 141, 142, 143,
        154, 159, 179, 181, 185, 186, 190
insurance fraud 115
intellectual property 5, 125, 126, 127, 128, 129, 174, 175
investments 183
IRA 95, 99, 181, 185, 191

J

joint accounts 48, 49
joint tax returns 20

L

life insurance 5, 27, 106, 107, 109, 110, 111, 112, 113, 114, 115, 148,
        181, 182, 185, 192
lifestyle 101, 105, 143
lifestyle analysis 21, 24, 25, 27, 181
Limited Liability Company 160, 164, 176
Limited Partnership 160, 164, 176
liquidating assets 103, 152
litigation 29, 33, 35
litigator 35
living expenses 3, 21, 25, 26, 134, 143, 194
lump-sum payment 96, 97, 103, 104, 105, 106, 107, 113

M

managing spouse 76, 77
marital assets 18, 26, 42, 51, 61, 73, 109, 119, 135, 136, 140, 141, 165
marital property 55, 56, 57, 62, 63, 64, 68, 69, 75, 79, 80, 81, 82, 94,
        95, 118, 119, 123, 127, 128, 158, 159, 161, 165, 172, 175, 177
mediation 29, 30, 31, 32, 33, 34, 35, 36
mortgages 18, 24, 48, 192, 193
MyFico 47, 48
MySpace 14

V

valuation date 69, 73, 74, 75, 76, 77

Y

year-end statements 18

Symbols

401(k) 63, 82, 94, 95, 98, 99, 181, 185, 191, 403(b) 95

Made in the USA
Lexington, KY
31 December 2013